Sacred Surprises

Sacred Surprises

DALE HANSON BOURKE

WORD PUBLISHING
Dallas · London · Vancouver · Melbourne

SACRED SURPRISES
WHEN GOD TURNS YOUR LIFE UPSIDE DOWN

Many of the names and some of the circumstances surrounding the events in this book have been changed in
order to protect the privacy of the people involved.

Scripture quotations are from The Holy Bible, New Inter-
national Version. Copyright © 1973, 1978, 1984
International Bible Society. Used by permission of
Zondervan Bible Publishers.

Library of Congress Cataloging-in-Publication Data:

Bourke, Dale Hanson.
    Sacred surprises : when God turns your life upside
down / Dale Hanson Bourke.
        p.   cm.
    ISBN 0-8499-0883-3
    1. Women, Christian—Religious life. 2. Bourke,
Dale Hanson. I. Title.
BV4527.B67   1991
248.8'43—dc20   91-21656
                                                 CIP

12349 AGF 987654321

Printed in the United States of America

To anyone who has lost a child or a parent,
a spouse, a friend or a dream,
may this book serve as a reminder
that God weeps with you.

Contents

Acknowledgments

Although this book bears my name as author, there are many, many others who deserve credit for helping me live through the events described here, as well as encouraging me to record them.

Thanks to:

My parents, who raised me with love and wisdom;

Tom, whose love has held me together through triumphs, tragedies, and the everyday stuff of life;

Chase and Tyler, who have let me tell their stories;

Margaret and Robert Bourke, loving in-laws and grandparents;

Becky Pippert, Chelly Grossman, Jill Briscoe, Sara Fortenberry, Peggy Campbell, Susan Munao, Vickie Smick, Colleen Townsend Evans, Wendy Goldberg, Laura Minchew, and Nancy Norris, who, along with others, have been encouraging, loyal friends even when I has at my worst;

Leslie Nunn, my colleague and friend who models grace and patience with me daily;

Laura Schramm, who so kindly pieced together my thoughts onto one computer disk and who radiates God's love in all that she does;

ix

"Bill," "Liz," and the others I couldn't name in this book who let God speak through them, and in doing so, changed my life;

Julie Talerico and Jane Struck, who have helped shape my thoughts and have encouraged me constantly as I sent them my rough, rough columns;

Jan Johnson, my wonderful editor and friend, who helped focus my thoughts and shape my words;

And all of my family at Word Publishing who lived with me though some difficult days, loved me enough to be more than professionals, and encouraged me, challenged me, and shaped me as a writer and a believer.

That is the great conversion in our life: to recognize and believe that the many unexpected events are not just disturbing interruptions of our projects, but the way in which God molds our hearts and prepares us for his return.

HENRI J. NOUWEN

OUT OF SOLITUDE

And we know that in all things God works for the good of those who love him, who have been called according to his purpose.

ROMANS 8:28

Prologue

Dear God,

You know how I feel about surprises. It's not that I hate them. It's that they undo me. Make me jittery and unsure of myself. I don't know where they've come from or where they will take me. I'm afraid of them.

I'm much more secure with schedules and lists and plans. Oh, how I love to plan! I like knowing where I'm going and how long it will take to get there. I love the confidence I get from planning the events of my day. I revel in the success I feel when I cross out one more project from my "to do" list.

You know all this about me, God. Isn't this the way you made me? Haven't you seen me scurrying around like a little ant building a hill, happily moving debris from one place to another?

Yes, I know I get too intense some times. Too worried about projects and not caring enough about others. Too worried about doing and not enough about becoming. I know that you have to work hard sometimes just to get my attention.

I know your surprises are for my own good. I resist them, beg to be spared them, and yet I always know that they are your way of changing me into the person you want me to be.

Give me the courage to want to be more like you. Save me from my foolish plans and inflexible schedules. From the need to see ten steps ahead before I plant my foot.

I'm taking a deep breath and reaching out to you. Go ahead, God. Surprise me.

1

Saved

I WAS BARELY SIX YEARS OLD when I first gave my heart to God. Today we have euphemisms for the act: becoming a believer, turning toward God, giving one's heart to Christ. But in those days, in my church, there was only one way to say it. I got saved.

I sat through Sunday school one cold winter morning listening to a visiting evangelist preach a hellfire-and-brimstone message that made us all squirm in our chairs. Some of the children went forward in response to the altar call. But I was stubborn even then. I stared down at my shiny black patent leather shoes and refused to let my feet walk toward the man. I didn't want to be saved *from* something. In my childish way, I knew I wanted more than a passport out of hell. I couldn't have named it then. I barely can now.

Still, I thought about the message all day. Despite the preacher's shouting, there was a quiet stirring in my soul. I wanted a "personal relationship with Jesus." It wasn't hell that had caught my attention. It was the man pictured on the front of my Rainbow Bible. He was the One I wanted to know. I lay in bed that night, unable to sleep. Finally I called out to my father downstairs. "I need to talk to you," I said.

"Tell me how to get saved," I remember asking as Daddy sat on my bed. He carefully explained that I needed to ask for forgiveness of my sins, acknowledge my belief in Jesus, and then ask him to come into my heart. I had heard this all before, but tonight it was different. Tonight I felt sure that I wanted to do this myself.

My father asked if I understood exactly what I was doing. He carefully repeated the steps I would take. And then he did a surprising thing: he kissed me and left my room.

"This is something between you and God," he said as he walked out. "I never want you to look back at this and think I had anything to do with it."

I felt abandoned. What if I prayed the prayer the wrong way? What if I didn't use the right words? I got down on my hands and knees beside my bed and prayed as best I could. I got back into bed and lay there for a few minutes. I didn't feel anything. Maybe the first prayer hadn't worked. I jumped out of bed and prayed again. I felt a little better. Finally, I hopped back into bed and drifted off to sleep.

The details of that experience have never left my mind, even after thirty years. I can still picture my father, younger than I am now, sitting on my bed in the shadows. And over the years I have marveled at the wisdom it took to say, "This is between you and God." It is a phrase I will never forget.

There are some who would say a six-year-old cannot possibly understand what it means to give her life to God. True, my theological understanding was minimal at best. I knew so little about life, how could I make a decision that had an impact on every aspect of it? But I still remember the stirring in my heart that day. It was something I had never felt before. Something sacred.

Over the years the importance of that commitment was overshadowed at times by other interests. It was as if I could still stare at my patent leather shoes and will God away. Sometimes I was too busy for him. Sometimes I knew he wouldn't like what I was up to. And sometimes he just didn't seem relevant to what I was doing. How quaint the notion of being saved seemed.

I thought I could get by with acknowledging God in the same way I declared my political party. And I did, for a long time. I didn't deny God. I stood up for him. But I didn't thirst for him. I didn't want his will to be done unless it happened to go along with my will.

I remember telling someone, "Yes, God is an important part of my life." I can hear those words, almost see the expression on my face, which was calculated to be neither intimidating nor pious. But now those words cut through me and cause me pain. Yes, God was a *part* of my life. How blasphemous that

I thought I could keep him there. How foolish that I didn't realize he was the very definition of my life.

And so he waited in the wings. And I carried on stubbornly, nodding to him now and then. I was in control of my life. Everything was going well. We had reached an accommodation of sorts that seemed to be working for me. That is, until the foundation of my carefully constructed world began to crack.

Looking back now, I see my arrogance clearly. My gospel was my "to do" list. If I could accomplish enough, move forward fast enough, and keep everything under my control, I would be fine. I had a sign on my desk that said, "I hate surprises." It was a reminder to the other people in my office that I needed a little warning if things weren't going as planned. My organized nature was undone by the unexpected.

But the unexpected happened to me, just as it happens to all of us at one time or another. Not just a little upset of plans. The Unexpected that stole the very core of what we think we know. The Unexpected that strips away pretense and pride. The Unexpected that either destroys or becomes the soil of new growth.

God surprised me. He shook me. And then he gathered me into his arms and held me there. "It is just between us," he reminded me gently. And as I looked into his face, I knew that this lesson would not be forgotten.

Doubt eats away the old relationship with God, but only so that a new one can be born. . . . One thing is certain, that passage through the darkness of doubts and crises, however painful they may be, is essential to growth in the process of faith.

JOHN POWELL
A REASON TO LIVE! A REASON TO DIE!

Save me, O God,
for the waters have come up to my neck.
I sink in the miry depths,
where there is no foothold.
I have come into the deep waters;
the floods engulf me.
I am worn out calling for help;
my throat is parched.
My eyes fail,
looking for my God.

PSALM 69:1–3

Dear God,

The pain is too great for me to bear. I always thought I was a strong person. But now I know. I have just been spared the pain that would have shown me how weak I am.

I am broken, empty, shattered. I want to reach out to you, but I don't have the energy to even try. I need you now. Can you hear me?

I have learned not to fight the pain of childbirth. I have practiced going along with the waves of a contraction until they pass. Can I do the same with this pain? Fighting it hasn't helped. Can I learn to breathe through it?

I feel a strange inclination to turn toward the pain instead of run from it. Am I like the deer attracted to the shining headlights of the car that will kill her? Or are you trying to show me the way? Are you trying to tell me that there is something beyond the pain? There are many who say they speak for you, but their words bring me no comfort.

God, I know that this is just between the two of us. No one else can help me through this. I am alone except for you. And yet, I cannot see you or feel you through the suffering. I am too busy gasping for breath to call out your name.

Will I survive this? And if I do, who will I be?

Don't let me grow hard and cold, God. Don't let me go through this for nothing. Keep me open, God. Even to the pain. Especially the pain.

2

Free Fall

T HE ROOM WAS DARK AND COLD. Even now as I think of it I shiver involuntarily. But I didn't shiver then. Then I didn't move; I barely breathed. It was as if I believed that laying perfectly still would somehow rob the moment of its horrible reality. *This is not happening*, I remember saying to myself. It sounded as ridiculous then as it does now, but I said it in my mind anyway, over and over and over again.

I didn't feel the cold. I didn't feel anything at all. I was not afraid or angry or panicked. *This is what it is like to skydive*, I thought. *This is how they describe a free fall*. I don't know why I thought of parachuting at a moment like that. But now I see that I had just begun my free fall. I was floating without control. I didn't even know if I had a rip cord. It didn't seem to matter.

Eventually I prayed. At least I did what I had been taught to do; what passed for prayer in those days. My prayer was more like my opening position in a negotiation. I hadn't yet learned that God didn't believe in collective bargaining. *Things like this don't happen to*

15

people like me, I pointed out rationally. *I do my part; I obey the rules. Now you're supposed to do your part.* I waited for his response, but I heard nothing.

Make this all a dream, I asked, trying not to sound demanding. *Let it be a mistake. Let the doctor come in here and tell me that the equipment is wrong or the nurse is inexperienced.* I waited. Still nothing.

I searched my memory for answers. Wasn't this the moment when God was supposed to become more real than ever to me? I mentally flipped through Bible verses I had learned as a child. But the one that came to mind seemed inappropriate. It began to play over and over like a broken record: "He descended into hell. He descended into hell." I tried to block it out, but I had no energy or will power.

Finally I gave in. *Yes, this is what is happening to me*, I thought. *I am descending into hell.* And nothing has prepared me for this moment.

"After the first death there is no other," Dylan Thomas observed. For me it wasn't just the occasion of the first death that made it so hard. It was the life, my life, that had preceded it. It was an existence in which pain had been avoided or minimized or controlled. Now it was confronting me from all sides. I turned away from it and ran into it again. I turned inside and found nothing.

I lay there in that dark, cold room and stared at my stomach. It was enormous, almost ready to engulf me. It was still exposed, the skin stretched so tight I could see the network of veins. I traced their course

16

idly with my eyes. Finally I moved one hand, placing
it on the left side of my belly. I patted my baby, trying
to comfort him. Slowly I raised the other hand. I could
still feel her body; it didn't feel any different. I stroked
her gently, hoping to ease her journey. I thought of the
movie *Sophie's Choice* and the scene in which she had
to choose which of her children to turn over to the
Nazis. At least I hadn't been asked to make a choice.

The doctor said, "I'm sorry," but I seemed to hear
"It is finished." Still I had not been on this path long
enough to understand very much.

So I said, "Please take me to the hospital. Save my
other baby if you can."

My doctor looked at me and said gently but
clearly: "I am only a surgeon. Your baby is in God's
hands."

He was right. I knew that of course. But at that
moment he seemed to believe it far more than I. How can
I trust this baby to God when he just took my other child
from me? I wanted to scream. But I said nothing.

I had not chosen this doctor for his faith. I chose
him because he was a very good doctor. But I saw how
quickly he turned away from his own answers and
toward God. I was ashamed that I felt no such inclination. Where had all those years of Sunday school
brought me?

The doctor handed me a box of tissues, but I just
looked at them, not understanding what they were for.
Then I realized that I should be crying. I knew this, but
still I felt nothing.

I said, "Thank you," but could not force a tear from my eyes. "We need to do something," I said, still not understanding.

"Go home and rest," the doctor suggested. "Call your husband and have him take you home. Tomorrow I'll have you see a specialist." I listened to the words carefully, letting them echo in my head. He was telling me to do nothing, to just wait. It was a sentence I was not ready to hear. I was used to doing things, to controlling situations.

The patients were lining up in the waiting room. I knew that the doctor had to go on to others. But I had to ask, I had to know: "Why did it happen? Did I do something wrong? Could I have prevented it?"

My kind doctor shook his head. "I know it's not easy, but we'll probably never know. We can order an autopsy, but even then we may never know. I doubt any of us could have done anything to prevent it. Babies die. Sometimes we forget that every birth is a miracle."

He was talking about God again. I wanted him to give me technical answers, to suggest surgery, to give me statistics. But instead he reminded me that God was in control. I was not comforted by that fact. If God was in control, why had he allowed my baby to die? Why had he created her, let her grow happily beside her twin brother, and then taken her before I could know her, before she could know life outside my womb? Was he trying to punish me? To teach me something? Was this God so capricious that he didn't even need a reason?

I called my husband's office, but he was in a meeting. "No, don't bother him," I said. *He couldn't do anything anyway,* I thought. I'll just handle this for now. I was good at handling things.

Walking out of the doctor's office I was shocked that it was still a beautiful, sunny August day. People were going about their business as usual. I wanted to tell them to stop. My world had just turned upside down, and no one seemed to notice. I stepped onto the hot pavement, but there was no sensation of heat or pressure on my feet. I was so disconnected; I felt as if I were floating. My body knew what to do, but my mind seemed unable to comprehend or control the motions.

The heat of the car made me recoil as I opened the door. I had been so cold just moments before. I remembered that. Now I was so hot. *Wait before you get in,* a voice inside my head said. *Leave the door open, turn the key, start the air conditioner.* I did it all in slow motion. *Now drive carefully,* the voice said again. Taking my usual route home I saw the grocery store ahead. Signalling conscientiously, I pulled into the parking lot. It was something to do. I needed something to do.

As I walked through the familiar aisles I grabbed for staple foods. It was what my mother and I had done when we heard predictions of a snowstorm. Milk, bread, butter, eggs, and meat. Those were the things you needed in a time of crisis. If you couldn't shovel your way out of the driveway, you needed to be able to survive.

19

I didn't know what storm was coming my way, but survival was my only objective. Whatever happened to me or my other baby, I still had to get food for my husband, Tom, and Chase, my four-year-old. If I could do nothing for the babies I carried inside of me, I still could be a mother to my son.

At the checkout counter a teenage boy was bagging the groceries.

"Wow. You must be having twins!" he said, eyeing my stomach.

I had heard the comment often over the past months as my body stretched and contorted to accommodate the two babies. But now I wasn't expecting two babies. One was dead. The other might die soon. The boy looked at me, waiting for my response.

"Yes," I said in a voice that seemed to echo.

His cheerful young face smiled.

"I thought so," he said, winning the bet with himself.

My face smiled back involuntarily, sparing him the harsh truth. Perhaps he could live a few more years without knowing that life was not what it seemed. Maybe he'd never have to learn that sometimes babies die on sunny August days. And that just when you need God the most, he can seem so far away that you wonder if he was ever there at all.

3

Chase's Sister

W ALKING INTO THE HOUSE that day, everything
seemed the same for a moment. Had it been a
dream? My son was taking his nap, and the babysitter
sat watching a soap opera. I stood and stared at the
screen for a few minutes. Perhaps I had expected that
real-life crises would happen like they did on soap
operas. That there would be a sense of foreboding and
ominous music before anything really important
occurred. I searched my memory for clues I might
have overlooked.

Certainly the news that we were expecting twins
had taken us by surprise. But Tom and I had moved
from shock to awe when we first saw the two tiny
babies on the ultrasound screen. We had prepared
ourselves as best we could for the addition of two
children. *Was there a moment when we had resented the
idea?* I wondered. *Was God punishing us for an idle
thought or a selfish wish?* I shook my head, trying to
clear my thinking. *This is crazy*, I said to myself. *God
doesn't do things that way.* I knew I would have been the

first to tell that to someone else, but I wasn't so sure I believed it myself. I didn't know what I believed anymore.

I had to stop thinking so much. I had to do something. I picked up the telephone and dialed the church.

"I need to speak to the minister," I said, hoping he would do what his title implied.

"Is it an emergency?" the woman on the other end of the line asked efficiently, expecting to dismiss my call.

"Yes," I said simply.

I wanted to say more. I wanted to tell her that my baby had died and I was afraid I had lost my faith, too. I wanted to sound vulnerable and needy, but instead I sounded brusque. *What kind of emergency could it be?* she must have wondered.

She put me on hold. A minute ticked by, and I considered hanging up. What would I say to this man I hardly knew? I thought of his young face compared to the wise older man who had just retired from our church. How could I tell this man that no sermon had prepared me for this emptiness?

Finally I heard the pastor's voice.

"I'm sorry to bother you," I said. I had been taught to always be polite. At least my manners had not failed me. Briefly, I explained the situation. "What should I do?" I asked him.

"Put it behind you," he responded.

I asked about a service, a burial. I was pushing now, showing him that I was not yet ready to put it behind me.

But he heard none of my pain. "If it's important to you, we can schedule a service. Why don't you call back when you have more details?"

He's a busy man, I said to myself. *Don't ask too much.* But I felt something for the first time since I lay in that dark, cold room. Was it anger? Not quite. Later I would feel anger. Later I would want to go to him and say, "I needed you, and you let me down." But by that time I would be far enough down the road to realize that I wasn't ready to be helped even if he had offered it. I will forgive him without him ever realizing his need for it.

As I hung up the phone, I was surprised by its ring. Picking it up again I heard the familiar voice of my husband.

"Are you alone?" I ask.

I tell him that I have some bad news, trying to prepare him, trying to make it easier on him than it was on me. Or maybe I am just trying to find a way to control what I can. Calmly I tell him what I know and what I don't. His response is immediate—a gasp and a promise to come right home. I am sorry for the pain I hear in his voice, for the raw nerves that are so easily exposed. I am sorry that I still feel nothing myself.

"Mommy?" a sleepy voice calls to me. My four-year-old has awakened from his nap. I have been trying to wean him of this afternoon ritual in anticipation of school in the fall, but today I am grateful for the time he has had to blissfully escape the world. He comes over to me and hugs my middle, by now accustomed to the bulk that separates us.

"Hi babies," he says, rubbing my tummy.

My sweet, loving child has already grown attached to the brother and sister he has been expecting and praying for each night. How will I tell him without destroying his spirit? He is too young to know about death. He has not even had the chance to learn about birth.

Chase and I snuggle together, and I find his touch comforts me in a way I have never before experienced. For the first time I need him more than he needs me. I hold onto him for strength and courage. And slowly I begin to feel the pain. Telling Chase what has happened will be the most difficult moment for me. Explaining the inexplicable will challenge me as a mother more than anything I have ever imagined. My eyes feel hot, my throat dry. I know that the tears are finally coming. I will them away until Tom comes home, until we can tell Chase together that our lives have changed and that our dreams must be altered.

"Are you okay, Mommy?" the high-pitched voice asks.

"Yes, honey," I assure him. "I was just thinking about how much I love you."

"I love you, too," he says, hugging me and the babies at the same time.

When Tom comes home we spend a moment talking and grieving. And then we know we must tell Chase. "Don't tell children more than what they want to know," I remember reading somewhere. I had planned to use this advice when it came time to talk about sex. But I must use it today.

Tom begins slowly.

"Remember that we told you we were going to have two babies?" he asks Chase gently.

"Yes," Chase acknowledges.

"Well now we're only going to have one," Tom says, and I pray that he is right, that we will still have one baby when it is all over.

"Why?" Chase asks, no longer calm.

"Because one of the babies died," I tell him as quietly as I can.

"Was it my brother or my sister?" he asks immediately. I am startled by his understanding, by the fact that these babies are as real to him as they are to me.

"It was your sister," I say. And now I cannot hold back the tears. It was my baby girl, Chase's baby sister, the daughter we had dreamed of for months.

"Oh no!" Chase wails. "Is my baby brother all right?"

I try to assure him that the other baby is fine, but I am not so sure. We don't know what happened to our baby girl; the same evil could be attacking our baby boy. I want to reassure Chase, but I also want to prepare him for more bad news.

"Was she sick?" Chase asks. I don't understand his question at first and then I realize that he, too, wants to know why.

"Yes, honey, she was probably sick," I say.

27

"Then why didn't we give her medicine?" Chase presses.

I want to explain it all to him, but I don't have answers. I should know what to say to my own child, but I have already run out of answers after only four years in this role. I am not supposed to tell him more than he wants to know, but he wants to know everything. *Why would God do this to a child so young with a heart so tender?* I want to ask. But there is no place to go with my questions. I hug Chase as my tears fall onto his curly hair.

4

Waiting

W E ARE SITTING IN ANOTHER waiting room on yet another day. Each day of the last week has been spent in a different doctor's office or hospital waiting room. I have been examined and reexamined. My arm has been poked so many times that it has turned shades of blue and purple. I am learning to listen carefully while doctors talk about me and my babies as if I am not there. I am learning that the questions I ask rarely have clear answers.

Each specialist seems to have a different idea of what should be done with me. One wants to deliver my surviving baby. Another thinks we should wait until I go into labor naturally. A doctor insists that I should take steroids to help my baby boy grow quickly. Another doctor thinks it's too risky. I learn new terms and new statistics. And always I wait.

It is this waiting that is the worst for me. I want to do something. I want to know. But as the days stretch into weeks, I discover that I am trapped in a nightmare of powerlessness. I have no control over any aspect of my life. All I do is wait.

At night I cannot sleep. I have to be reassured constantly that there is still one life within me. I touch him through my own stomach, nudge him until I feel some spontaneous movement. I talk to him.

"Hold on," I say. "Please hold on."

I pat him and massage him, wondering if he misses the movement of his twin. Wondering if in some way he, too, is grieving the loss.

Sitting in one more waiting room, I begin to fill out one more form. Today there are new questions that I can't answer. Wearily, I turn to my husband for help. He is confused, too. We are both tired of the paperwork and protocol that pushes aside our sorrow. We have learned to drag ourselves through the process in the hope that someone will give us an answer instead of more questions.

"Maybe I can help you," a woman sitting next to us says kindly. I look at her and see that she is quite young, but her face looks wrinkled and haggard.

She reads the question. "Don't worry about that. You're not going to stay in the hospital overnight are you?" she asks.

I shake my head.

"The hospital doesn't need this if you're just an outpatient," she says knowledgeably.

I notice the bag she has beside her that contains knitting, a book, and a soft drink. She is obviously used to the hospital routine.

"Why are you here?" she asks.

I tell her briefly about my babies, one dead, the other alive. I have learned to give a simple description of the trauma that has come to define our lives. I have learned that most people do not want to look at me once they know. They do not want to see my huge stomach, realizing that it represents both hope and despair. But this woman is different.

"I'm so sorry," she says, grasping my arm. I see tears in her eyes and I understand that she is not just being polite.

"Are you waiting to see a doctor, too?" I ask.

"No," she says. "I'm waiting for my son. He's having chemotherapy."

Her words are just sinking in when a little boy appears in the waiting room. He is slightly older than Chase. A baseball cap does little to disguise his bald head. His translucent skin barely covers his bones. A tube is inserted into his tiny chest. I am so horrified by the sight of this walking skeleton that I almost cry out. The mother in me wants to hug him, but part of me recoils. I realize that my reaction to him is not unlike how some people respond to me. Tragedy makes us uncomfortable; reminds us that our own world is vulnerable. I have learned this lesson, and yet the thought that this boy could be Chase undoes me. How could I bear to watch my child suffer?

"Hi Mom," he calls in a raspy voice. "Ready to go?"

"Sure, pal," she responds cheerfully. "Let me just gather up some things."

I watch the interaction with confusion. Their words are incongruously casual. But clearly this boy is as sick as any child I have ever seen.

"Tommy has leukemia," the woman explains as she places a book in her bag. "We spend a lot of time in waiting rooms."

She says it as if she is telling me that he plays Little League baseball, not announcing a death sentence. Now it is my turn to cry. I bite my lip, trying not to sob in front of the little boy.

"Good luck," she says to me as she puts her arm around her son.

I fight for air, wanting to tell her something that may help.

"God bless you," I say, surprising myself.

It is not simply a cliché. I want desperately for God to bless her and her son. To relieve some of the pain they must feel, to grant them more days together. I call on him on her behalf. It is more than an old habit. I watch them walk away together and I wonder how many more days God will give them.

I lay in bed that night, not sleeping again. The image of the woman and her dying child haunt me. I think of her kindness to me and wonder where she found the reserves to reach out to someone else when her own life contained so much pain.

I think of all the people I know who have gone through suffering. Some have become bitter and hard, their faces etched with frustration and anger. Others have a kindness and sensitivity that is almost

34

otherworldly. *When this is all over, what will I be like?* I wonder. *Will I be bitter and cold?*

"Oh God, keep me open," I cry. It is a selfish prayer in one way. I do not want to grow into an angry old woman. But in another way, it is the most honest prayer I have ever prayed. I am broken by the loss, by the waiting, by the uncertainty. I have no reserves left, no delusion of control. I ask only to keep from building a wall completely around me.

I think of another night when I called upon God. I was just a child then. I came with an open heart and my whole life ahead of me. Now I come with a heart that has been torn apart and a life that has been lived on my terms. It is harder now to ask God in. I have learned too well how to keep him out.

"Keep me open," I pray again, knowing that God is there and that he will answer. Knowing that my life will never be the same again.

Tyler Jackson Bourke was born September 8, 1988, three weeks after his twin sister died. Chase named his sister Joanna.

The question is not whether the things that happen to you are chance things or God's things because, of course, they are both at once. . . . Listen for him. Listen to the sweet and bitter airs of your present and your past for the sound of him.

FREDERICK BUECHNER
THE SACRED JOURNEY

"Now my heart is troubled, and what shall I say? 'Father, save me from this hour'? No, it was for this very reason I came to this hour. Father, glorify your name!"
JOHN 12:27–28

Dear God,

The world is full of pain. How could I have missed it for so long? How did I ignore the tense faces, the broken bodies, the hopeless sighs? Have they been there all along and I just ignored them?

I have become a magnet for those in pain. Every conversation I have lately comes around to loss. Everyone has lost someone or something. Some people seem to feel they have lost you.

God, I am still in need myself. Yet I am so drawn to the needy. I find some strange comfort with those who grieve.

The world has not changed, has it? The change is in me. You are drawing me to the pain, and for the first time I am not running away. I am turning toward the pain because I want to, not because it seems like a good thing to do. I am turning toward the pain and I am finding you.

5

Women Never Forget

G REAT TO SEE YOU!" MY OUTGOING friend says as she gives me a hug. We have not seen each other for a year. I think back to our last meeting and realize suddenly that a year ago I didn't even know I was pregnant. A year ago I knew so little about life and death. A year ago I was a different person.

"It's been a long time," I say. In every conversation now I search for lines to tie me down, to bring me back to the real world. I am too often floating; detached from the mundane by the tragic.

"How's your new job?" I ask, willing myself toward reality.

"Terrific!" she says enthusiastically. And then she gingerly moves the conversation toward me. "You look good."

I laugh as I thank her for the attempt. I am carrying the extra weight from a twin pregnancy and months in bed. I do not look good at all. I know she means I look good considering what I've been through, but she is too polite to say it.

We sit down and order coffee. The silence hangs between us uncomfortably. We are usually talking over one another, catching up on the news of ourselves and mutual friends. But I have little news to offer. Tyler is a wonderful, easy baby. I try to think of what you tell people about newborns. All I can think of is how grateful I am that he is alive and healthy. And how he comforts me when the tears come for his sister.

"I was really sorry to hear about your baby," my friend says, broaching the subject that she fears. Looking for common ground she offers, "My sister lost a baby. It took her a long time to get over it."

I listen to her words and try to appreciate her kindness. But I wonder if she understands that her sister has never "gotten over it." She may have learned to hide her pain, to get on with life, to avoid the topic. But I doubt she has forgotten. Women who have lost babies never forget.

I used to think they did. I thought it strange that a young healthy woman would grieve for months over a miscarriage. *Why doesn't she just try again?* I would ask in my mind. I didn't understand then that the loss was more than physical. I didn't understand that even if the woman went on to have six children, she'd always wonder about the one that she lost.

But now I have joined a sorority that I never knew existed. We are the women who have a memorial in our hearts for our own flesh. We will visit occasionally, adding bouquets as the years go by. Others will think we have gone on with our lives, and they will be right. We have gone on, but we are not the same.

We will always know that happiness is fleeting, that life has no promises. We are the ones who will pass a pregnant stranger and offer up a prayer for her and her baby. We are the ones who will watch a sad movie and cry much longer than we should. We are the ones who will sit in the midst of a happy family scene with a smile on our faces and a sad look in our eyes. We are the ones who know that every healthy baby is a miracle.

We come in all shapes and ages. Most people never suspect who we are. But when we hear of another woman's loss, we remember. And we are compelled to touch this woman, to ease her way into the group none of us wanted to join.

We know that it is the touch of another woman that can hold us together at that point. It was the touch of my friend Chelly, who had anguished over the loss of her own baby, that allowed me to cry tears of true sorrow. When she said, "I understand," I believed her. As she cried with me, I knew she was ripping open her own wounds. When she spoke about God, she helped me believe that he was still there; that he had, in fact, sent her to do his work.

It was the warmth in the formal note from the woman down the street, a woman with grandchildren, who wrote: "It has been more than thirty years, but I still mourn the loss of my baby." I read her words over and over, wondering when the pain will finally become bearable. Will it take thirty years?

47

It was the touch of a familiar clerk in a department store who, in the middle of racks of clothes, hugged me and began to cry. She told me about her own two babies, one who had lived a few hours after birth, the other lost early in her pregnancy.

"It still hurts," she said. "I'll never forget them."

None of us will ever forget, whether we lost a baby last week or years ago. We remember every time we see a young child and wonder if ours would have looked like her. We remember when we look at our family pictures and wonder what it would have been like to have another little face in the portrait. We remember as we give away still usable highchairs and baby clothes, thinking they would have been worn out now if another little person had used them.

"Have another baby," people recommend after a loss. They mean well, but they don't understand that there is a unique place in a mother's heart for each child she conceives. Another child will never fill that empty place, just as the years will never take away the memory.

It is a memorial to the dreams that were never replaced by reality. Those what-might-have-beens hang out there forever, taunting a mother's desire to nurture and protect, to encourage and defend. The child she cannot hold holds her captive, leaving her always to wonder.

Most women who have lost babies learn to hide their scars. They realize it is not acceptable to mourn too long or bear their pain too openly. But that does not mean they forget. Women who have lost babies never forget.

6
Brokenhearted

WALKING INTO THE OFFICE, I greet this man I have never met before and try to seem professional. On the outside I am dressed like a businesswoman. I carry a briefcase and wear a suit. I shake hands and observe professional courtesy. But on the inside I am still raw. At any moment I may cry, destroying my image and leading people to speculate about my sanity.

I should be getting over this, I tell myself. Life goes on. My time of grieving should be over. But it is not. Sometimes I wonder if it will ever be.

"I'm Bob Seiple," the man says. "Welcome to World Vision." I notice that he has kind eyes. His face is young; too young to be president of such a large organization. We chat for a few moments about the friends we have in common. I tell him I have come to learn more about his charity; he tells me that the organization works in nearly a hundred countries, sponsoring a million children. I am impressed by the statistics, but feel strangely disconnected. I breathe in and out carefully. I do not want to fall apart in this man's office.

But there is more. This man cares about the people he is talking about. I see in his eyes that he, too, is capable of crying. He tells of holding children in his arms, knowing that they will not live another day. He remembers mothers begging for food, not for themselves but for their babies.

Then he turns the conversation back to me.

"Didn't I hear that you have twins?" he asks.

The question takes my breath away. I have been asked before, and I have learned to recite a response: "I was expecting twins, but we lost our baby girl. I have a baby boy." Most people offer a quick condolence and move on. But not this man.

"I'm sorry to hear that," he says. He pauses just a moment before he continues. "Did you know that forty thousand babies die every day in the world?"

For a moment I think I will break down right here in front of this man. Doesn't he know how painful my loss is? How could he be so insensitive? But slowly, his words find their way through my own filter of grief. Forty thousand babies like mine. And forty thousand mothers. Women who have to bury their precious children, some with their own hands. Women who have little hope that the next child they bear will survive. Women who know exactly how I feel.

I look at this man again and know that he is neither insensitive nor cruel. He has handed me the words that God gave him.

"I want to help," I say, surprising myself by the evenness of my tone.

As I speak I feel new strength. For the first time in months I can think of going beyond my own grief. I want to help these women who suffer. I want to try to help save another baby's life.

Leaving his office, I feel a strange sensation. It is not quite happiness; it is hope. Hope for the women and children of the world. Hope for my own recovery. Hope that something good can come from pain.

I walk into the lobby and sit down for a moment to contemplate what has just happened. God has spoken through this man. He has thrown me a lifeline. He has not said, "Stop grieving." He has said, "Now you can understand." I feel myself begin to unfold. Instead of holding my grief inside, I begin to see it as a way to reach out. My grief is forming a bridge to others.

Looking up, I see the motto of the organization written on the wall: LET MY HEART BE BROKEN BY THE THINGS THAT BREAK THE HEART OF GOD. For the first time I realize that God grieves for my baby. And he grieves for all the others who have died, too.

Do I dare ask for a broken heart when I know how much it hurts? Am I willing to multiply my sorrow? I take a deep breath and pray, "Let my heart be broken . . ." But instead of pain I feel comfort. I no longer mourn alone.

7

Angel in Disguise

W E HAD NOTHING IN COMMON. I could tell from the minute I looked over at the woman seated next to me on the early morning flight to Chicago. She was wearing tight jeans, high heels, and a revealing blouse. Her hair was teased and sprayed; her makeup included several shades of eye shadow. She looked up from her copy of *Cosmopolitan* and smiled as I sat down.

"Where are you going this morning?" she asked in a rural Southern accent.

"Milwaukee," I replied, not wanting to start a conversation. I had work to do on the flight, and I didn't want to encourage small talk.

"I'm going to Green Bay," she said, without waiting for me to ask.

"Nice city," I said, hoping she'd consider it the benediction to our conversation. I pulled out my briefcase and began shuffling papers.

"Fly much?" she asked.

I took a deep breath and, bordering on rudeness, said, "I guess so."

"Boy, I sure don't. Hate to fly. I'm scared of crashing. Every time I hear a noise on an airplane, I have a fit."

I looked at her again and this time saw the fear in her eyes.

"Don't worry," I said, trying to adopt an official tone. "This is an easy flight and it's a clear day. Why don't you read something to take your mind off of it?" I suggested.

She seemed to take the hint, and I went back to my work. But a moment later my concentration was broken by the loud cracking of her gum. It continued as I leafed through several pages, and I found myself rereading each sentence to the staccato rhythm of her snapping.

By the time breakfast was served, I had accomplished next to nothing. "Make her be quiet," I prayed peevishly. After all, I was trying to do "Christian work." It seemed that God could be called upon to help me out.

"Nothing for me," she said to the stewardess. "I'm too nervous to eat." She smiled at me, but didn't say a word. I could still see the fear in her eyes, and, for the first time noticed something else, too. There was a certain sadness about her, a fatigue that was barely masked by the bright colors on her face. The distance between us seemed to lessen as I began to sense her pain.

"Where are you from?" I asked with a sense of resignation. I knew that I was about to hear the woman's life story.

She talked for several minutes about her small hometown and her dreams of a better life in a big city. As I looked at her clothes again, I realized that she had probably dressed in her best imitation of sophistication. She suddenly looked like a child playing dress up.

"Would you like to see a picture of my son?" she asked. I nodded, and she pulled out several pictures of a handsome teenager. I looked at her more closely, but decided that she couldn't be much more than thirty herself.

"You're so young . . ." I began, and she laughed.

"Yep. I was just a baby myself when I had him. Ran off with my high school sweetheart and next thing we knew, we had a baby."

I watched her face as she smiled and talked about the first days of her marriage. There was no pain in the memories, only happiness and wonder. But she wore no wedding ring, and I sensed that something had happened after those early years.

"He's dead now," she said abruptly. "He was such a good person. I still don't understand why he had to die." There were tears in her eyes as she told me about the car accident that had killed him two years before.

I felt tears forming in my own eyes as I listened to her describe the disbelief, the anger, and the sorrow that had driven her to a nervous breakdown following his death.

"I just gave up on everything," she said simply. "Myself, other people, even God."

"Why are you listening to me talk about this?" she asked suddenly. "Most people don't want to hear about people dying. They try to change the subject. That's the hardest part. No one wanted to talk to me after a while, because all I wanted to talk about was death."

"I think I understand a little bit about how you feel," I said. "Before I lost a baby I didn't like to hear anyone talk about pain. It scared me. But now I sometimes feel like I'm drawn to people who are hurting."

"Did you give up on God, too?" she asked.

Looking at her for a minute, I knew it was important to tell the truth.

"I felt like he was very far away," I told her honestly. "Nothing seemed to make sense to me. But I continued to pray for one thing. I asked God to make me more open, not to let me become hard or cold."

"Did it work?" she asked.

I looked at my new friend and smiled.

"Yes," I said, hugging her. "It worked."

Some readers may find this story familiar. It first appeared in *Everyday Miracles* in 1989. I include it here because this woman, truly one of God's brokenhearted, touched my life in a profound way.

8

Blessed Are the Poor

F IRST I HEARD THE WHIMPERING of a small child. I
looked up from my shopping list and spotted him
slumped in the seat of the shiny cart. His hair was
unkempt, his shirt dirty. His face was streaked with
tears that slid down his cheeks and dripped from his
chin. His little chest moved up and down as he tried to
suppress his sobs.

I was about to ask him if he was all right when a
woman rushed over from the nearby dairy counter.

"Shut up!" she hissed.

I stood in shock as I realized that this was his mother.

He whimpered again as she glared at him, and she
raised her hand in what seemed to be a well-practiced
gesture. Moving slightly toward them, I came into her
view. She glared at me, then at him, but dropped her
hand. He was safe for now, but her demeanor suggested that as soon as they were out of the sight of
strangers she would gladly follow through with her
threatened slap, punishment for nothing more than
expressing his feelings.

I wanted to hug the boy, to protect him, but as she jerked the shopping cart around and wheeled toward the checkout line I stood motionless. "Stop!" I wanted to yell. But instead I realized that I, too, was beginning to cry right in the middle of the gleaming supermarket. I cried for the little boy and his pain, for the woman and the frustrations that had driven her to act hatefully toward her own child, and for all of the people in the grocery store who were surrounded by so much and yet had so little.

I had just returned from a trip to Latin America with World Vision, and the shock of reentry into American society was a fresh wound. Everywhere I turned I was amazed by the abundance of *things*. In this grocery superstore, for example, I stood and stared at the produce department for several minutes, suppressing the desire to gather up the gleaming fresh apples and send them in a box to the children I had seen begging on the streets of Guatemala City just a few days before.

I wondered what they would think of this store that offered me more than a dozen choices of breads, milk with every variation of butterfat, and a meat department that stretched the entire length of the store. Could they even conceive of such wealth?

I looked at the rack of reduced items and thought that the people I had seen living in the city dump would have found any one of these items to be an unimaginable treasure. Overripe fruit and dented cans would have seemed like delicacies to them.

But it was the little boy and his mother who shocked me the most upon my return to the land of plenty. I had been prepared to see the poverty of Latin America; what I hadn't expected was the wealth. In a week of visiting the poorest of the poor, I had never seen a child mistreated. Despite physical discomfort, hunger and disease, there was a love of the children that seemed almost reverent. Mothers beamed as they presented their children to visitors. Adults gladly shared their meager resources with the young.

Yet here, in this supermarket, surrounded by wealth, I saw a woman poorer than any poor I had met on my trip. I wanted to tell her that her child would be better off in Guatemala, where he might go without shoes or three meals a day, but chances are, he would be loved. I wanted her to see what she was doing to herself and her son. But instead I just wept.

I know that the supermarket wasn't any different since my last visit. I'd probably heard mothers yell at their children before and simply ignored them. But *I* was different. I had seen wealth in spirit amidst material poverty. Now I recognized true poverty more clearly even when it was disguised by wealth.

I was struggling to understand this when I picked up Henri Nouwen's book, *Gracias*. "Wealth takes away sharp edges of our moral sensitivities and allows a comfortable confusion about sin and virtue," he wrote. His words struck me with painful intensity. What a price we pay for comfort, I realized.

65

Each day that I spend back in my cozy home, driving in my temperature-controlled car, eating meals that leave me more than full takes me further away from the clarity I experienced in a land of need. I know that I do not have to take a vow of total poverty to experience this purity again. But I do know that the poor are truly blessed.

Their vision is not blurred by the numbing abundance I experience each day. They never ask for more; they only dream of enough. I have more than I can ever use—yet talk regularly about my "needs." How God must grieve over my foolishness.

9

Blessed Are the Prisoners

I T WASN'T ANYTHING LIKE THE way I spend most of my Saturdays. Instead of running errands and attending soccer games, I found myself in a field under a tent at something that resembled a pep rally and worship service rolled into one.

The circumstances were unusual, and the location was even stranger. I was in the middle of the largest women's prison in the world. I had come to hear Chuck Colson speak and to observe the work of Prison Fellowship volunteers. Beyond that I didn't know what to expect.

My first surprise was that it seemed so hard to get into the prison. My identity was checked and rechecked. I was told to leave my purse in the car. I had to beg to bring in a pencil and small notebook. Three doors clanked shut before I entered the prison yard.

Once inside, my first thought was that these women look more normal than I thought they would. None wore uniforms. Groups gathered under trees or at tables, chatting. On the surface, many looked happy, almost carefree. I puzzled over that for a moment. Had I expected worry, sadness, hostility? Could it be that there was little they could worry about and less they could do? They had few choices to make each day and there was little they could do to change their circumstances. I almost asked one of the women I passed if she knew anyone in prison with a "to do" list.

The closer I looked, the more I was aware of the eyes of these women behind bars. Many reflected anger and coldness. Some seemed hopeless and dazed. Others were suspicious.

"What do you want with us?" they seemed to ask.

I wanted to say, "We've come to help," but I was too intimidated. And besides, I wasn't even sure that was true or what help would mean. I had come as much out of curiosity as evangelistic concern.

The gathering for the service was large. Nearly two hundred inmates filed in and sat on folding chairs set up on the ground floor. Women serving as ushers walked up and down the aisles, pointing to available seats. Each carried a roll of toilet paper. *Why would that be?* I wondered.

One by one, prisoners stood up to give their testimonies. They talked of lives lost and then found. Of crimes and punishment and then the release they experienced through faith. Some sang songs they'd written about the life they'd found through Jesus. Tears began to flow as the service continued. The women who carried the rolls of toilet paper hurried up and down the rows, offering pieces to the women who unself-consciously sobbed.

A woman named Linda stood up at the front and began to tell her story. She was attractive and articulate. She looked like she could live on my street or shop at my supermarket.

"I was trying to be the best wife and mother I knew how to be," she said. "That's how I ended up here, doing fifteen years to life."

She went on to say that she was grateful to be in prison because now she knew that she had to rely on Jesus. That controlling her life herself only brought her heartache and pain. I listened to her words and watched the other women nodding. I wanted to nod myself, but I was too self-conscious.

By now it was clear to me that I had come to this place to learn. The vibrancy of the testimonies and the vitality of these women's faith were unlike anything I'd seen on the outside.

As Chuck Colson spoke, there was almost an electricity in the air. Many of these women knew the Jesus he was talking about. They shouted "Amen" to his words and quoted verses right along with him.

My curiosity turned to amazement as I realized that these women, locked behind walls, without freedom or control over their lives, had the kind of vibrant faith that so many of us seek. Those of us who had come into the prison that day seemed spiritually anemic compared to these jailed believers.

I remembered my earlier thoughts about "to do" lists. Stripped of the clutter of daily life, these women had a clear sense of priorities. Humiliated in front of family and friends, they had no false sense of pride. Locked within fences and walls, they knew where to look for relief.

The three doors clanked behind me as I emerged from prison that day. I stopped for a moment, almost envious of what I was leaving behind. How easy it is for me to get caught up in all my choices and tangled by my freedom. How often I try to be the best wife and mother I can be, relying on my own strength instead of guidance from above. How foolishly proud I am of my "to do" list when I have scratched off one more item.

As I reflected on the extraordinary day, the Beatitudes began to run through my mind. Blessed are the poor, the meek, those who mourn . . .

"Blessed are the prisoners," I added. "For they shall know true freedom."

10

All That Glitters...

T HE CONFERENCE WAS ALMOST ready to begin, and I
searched the crowd for an empty seat. Finally
I spotted one on the aisle toward the front and slipped
in as quickly as I could. The man sitting to my right
smiled and held out his hand. "Pleased to meet you,"
he said congenially, and I smiled back as I introduced
myself, keenly aware that I didn't fit in here.

It was a meeting of the wealthy and successful. I
was here to report on the meeting, not as an invited
participant. Although I had dressed in my best clothes,
I felt shabby, an interloper in this group of immensely
wealthy individuals.

I had come to do a story, but I also had come here
to think. I had to make a decision by the end of the
week, and I planned to use the time when I wasn't
taking notes to carefully weigh the pros and cons of
my choice.

God had been working in my life. There was no
doubt about it. He had begun to heal my pain, to offer
me chances for growth. He had begun to seem real to

me in a way I had never experienced him before. I wanted desperately to know him better. And so when the letter appeared out of nowhere, I attributed it to God's hand.

How else would I have received such an incredible offer? I wasn't one of the leading candidates by a long shot, and yet a letter had come to me, inviting me to apply for the opportunity of a lifetime on a magazine that was a dream come true for any journalist. It was a chance to report on the rich and famous in a magazine that would showcase my efforts with fancy art and glossy paper.

Even more unbelievable was the fact that I had made the last cut, and now I had been offered the job. It didn't seem possible that I would be chosen from so many qualified applicants. Had God intervened so I would succeed? Was he allowing me this opportunity so I could afford to work for Christian clients who couldn't pay much?

And yet I was strangely troubled. I wanted to know God better. Could I stay true to that goal while showcasing luxury? I had just read a verse that seemed to question that: "Be very careful, then, how you live—not as unwise but as wise, making the most of every opportunity, because the days are evil."

I felt torn in two directions.

"Help me decide," I prayed simply as the conference got underway.

As I listened to the speaker, I couldn't help but notice the appearance of the man sitting next to me.

He wore a beautifully cut jacket, and on his wrist an expensive watch glittered. *This is the type of person who will read the magazine,* I thought. *I need to know more about what this person likes.*

At the next break the man and I began to talk. He casually mentioned his horse farm, his airplane, his rare sports car. I listened carefully, mentally noting the things he was interested in.

Then he turned the conversation to me, and I was embarrassed. My life didn't compare to his in any way. I briefly described my work, and he seemed surprisingly aware of the things I did.

"I know the magazine you're talking about," he said. "In fact, I've read your work."

Suddenly I remembered his last name. I'd heard it before. Yet this man was too young to be the person.

"Are you related to . . ." I began, and he laughed.

"He's my father," the man said, referring to a well-known religious leader. "Everyone knows him. That's part of the reason that I took a different route for my life," he said with a wry grin. "I still read all of the religious publications. But business is my thing."

He certainly seemed to be good at what he did. And as we talked, I realized that this man still professed an interest in God. He had combined wealth with Christianity. Maybe I could, too.

When the lunch break came, he invited me to sit at his table. I was grateful to be included. As we talked over our meal, he asked me questions about my faith. I told him honestly that I had spent many years in a casual relationship with God. But then I told him about the loss of my baby and the fact that God seemed to be pulling me back toward him in a way I had never experienced before.

I was shocked to see tears in the man's eyes when I finished speaking.

"I've been through a great deal lately," he said. "But I haven't been able to talk about it, because everyone thinks I've got it all together. After all, I am the son of a saint," he said. "People like to look at my success, but they don't know about the other side."

Lunch was concluding, but the man and I sat there for the next hour as he told me about the other side of his life. The heartaches with his rebellious children, the anger of his wife, the disappointment he'd caused his parents. His business was nearly bankrupt. His doctor told him that the stress was killing him. His heart couldn't take the strain.

As I listened to the horror of this man's life, I felt shocked. Just a few hours before I had looked at him and imagined that his life was perfect. Now I had heard about a tangled mess that seemed to have no end. *How could he have strayed so far from the principles his father had taught,* I wondered. *How could he have made such a mess of his life?*

When I left that day I promised to pray for him, and I meant it. I was heartbroken over this man who could tell no one about his pain. I began to pray as I drove home.

Then I realized that I'd been so caught up in his problems that I hadn't thought about my decision. What would I tell the man who needed to know if I would take the job?

"Be very careful, then, how you live . . ." The verse played over and over again in my head. And then I saw it. God had given me this man as an answer to my prayer. Yes, I could take the job, earn more money, learn about—and maybe live—the life of the rich and successful. But it was a seductive force. Could I withstand the pressure? This man, who had learned about God from an early age, had chosen another path. His life was a testimony to the destructive side of success.

"Thank you for teaching me such a profound lesson," I prayed. "Thank you for reminding me that every door isn't opened by you."

I didn't wait until the end of the week to make my decision. I sent the man a letter that day, thanking him for the offer, but declining. I had no qualms as I deposited the letter in the mailbox. The decision had been easier than I ever imagined it could be. God had been answering my prayer even as I prayed it.

Prayer is the humble answer to the inconceivable surprise of living.

"No eye has seen,
   no ear has heard,
      no mind has conceived
         what God has prepared for those
            who love him."

1 CORINTHIANS 2:9

Dear God,

This new thirst for you comes not from duty but from a deep loving I haven't felt before. I see you where I once ignored your presence. Help me to see you more.

I am so sorry that it took me so long. I am sorry for the grief I caused you and the time I wasted. I am sorry that I still slip back into old patterns.

How is it that you have such infinite patience with me? I am a grown woman, but I am still a baby. I have never learned some of the most basic lessons about following you.

I am so stubborn, so in love with my ways. And yet, I *am* in love with you more than ever. I know you see it. It's a mystery to me how I can learn to love you more and still fall into the same old patterns. I know better than to follow me. I want to follow you. Show me how.

11

Spring Cleaning

I 'D BEEN IGNORING THE EVIDENCE for weeks. Caught up in my busyness, I continued to drag sweaters out of my closet and wrap myself in wool long after everyone I knew had made the switch to cottons, linens, and light gabardines. Finally one day I knew I had to face the facts: spring had arrived, summer was on the way, and it was time to pack away the comfort of my woolens.

I wasn't dragging my feet just because I have always loved sweaters more than T-shirts. By acknowledging the end of winter I had to come to terms with spring cleaning, that annual ritual that seemed to overwhelm me more each year. It wasn't the cleaning that bothered me. It was the sorting out of my life, the taking stock of what would stay and what would go. These days I never seemed to have time to catch my breath. How could I stop long enough to evaluate what had outlived its usefulness?

I considered storing everything away and taking on the task next fall. But then I decided that I was being silly. *The children's clothes had to be sorted anyway, so I might as well take on my closet too,* my logical side reasoned. And then came the call from the Salvation Army announcing a pickup in my neighborhood on the following Monday. There was just no putting it off anymore.

So on a bright sunny Saturday, with the windows flung open and the birds chirping encouragement, I dragged a big box upstairs and attacked my closet. The first few victories were encouraging: into the box went a blouse that was hopelessly out of style, then a skirt that I hadn't been able to squeeze into for years. A sweater that had shrunk joined the meager pile.

But half an hour later I had made little more progress. *If I lose weight, these pants will be perfect,* I hedged. *This dress might work if I can find a scarf to match it. All this skirt needs is a new zipper . . .* Exhausted by my indecisions, I sat down in front of my closet and stared at the overstuffed racks.

Suddenly I spotted a shimmering blouse almost hidden behind the sweaters and jackets. It was still as stunning as the day I had first seen it displayed on a mannequin. I had fallen in love with it, and even the price of it couldn't dull my affection. I had gone back to look at it three or four times before finally deciding that I had to have it. Of course, by then I had justified the purchase in my mind over and over. *This blouse will "dress up" my dull business suit so I won't need a new dress. It's such good quality that it will last for years. I will probably wear it more than anything else because I'll feel so good in it.*

But there it sat in my closet, unworn, still bearing
the exorbitant price tag. And instead of being a source
of pride, it became a symbol of shame. The Salvation
Army box sat almost empty while my closet was
overflowing with clothes I didn't wear and a shimmering blouse that had seduced me.

"Oh God," I prayed. "Please help me."

I sat for a minute more, reflecting on my material-
ism. And then I slowly reached for the blouse and
carefully folded it up before placing it in the box.
Perhaps it would keep some poor person warm, I thought.

Feeling better, I went back to my task of sorting
the rest of my clothes. Then another thought came to
me. I remembered reading some advice about taking
everything out of your closet first and then putting
back only what you wear regularly. Grabbing armfuls
of clothes, I pulled everything out of my closet and
laid it on the bed. Suddenly my perspective was different. Instead of choosing castoffs I was selecting
favorites: the black skirt I wore at least once a week.
The white blouse that fit perfectly with every
jacket. The blue jeans that were my weekend uniform.
I selected a dozen items and then looked at the pile
still on the bed. *Did I really need any of it?* I wondered.

And then slowly I realized that God was teaching
me something that went beyond greed and material-
ism. I looked at my nearly empty closet and I thought
of my cluttered life. It was full of activities, some
good and meaningful, others frivolous and selfish.
Now and then the stress would become too great, and

I'd reluctantly offer an activity back to God. Sometimes I had to hand back something that had become too attractive to handle—an activity that began to define me more than I defined it. But God wanted more. I saw it as clearly as I now saw the racks in my closet.

So there, in front of my pile of clothes, I knelt and prayed.

"Take it all, God," I offered. "Put back into my life only what you want; only what is necessary."

It wasn't an easy prayer, but it felt like a fresh start. And as the breeze blew through the windows and the birds chirped along, I praised God that he was willing to do spring cleaning on my life.

12

The Moon

ON THE OCCASION OF HIS SECOND birthday, my son Tyler discovered the moon. We had gathered in the backyard to celebrate my youngest's birthday, and time slipped away as we talked and ate birthday cake. In fact, we didn't even notice Tyler for a while until we heard his gleeful shriek.

Standing in the middle of the yard, he was jumping up and down and pointing up.

"Light!" he exclaimed, searching his limited vocabulary for an appropriate word.

But he knew that didn't do it.

"Hot?" he asked, studying the glow that extended from the vibrant harvest moon.

The festivities stopped as we all went to view the source of Tyler's excitement. His round face was illuminated by the light of the moon, and he squealed as he pointed, excited by his discovery and delighted to be sharing it with his family. We laughed as we realized that Tyler had never been allowed to stay up late enough to see the moon. As far as he was concerned, it had never existed until that moment.

"Whas dat?" he asked me, taking his eyes off the object long enough to look at me imploringly.

"That's the moon," I said, rediscovering it myself.

"Moooon," Tyler tried, saying it with reverence. And then with delight he began to point again. "Moon! Moon!" he crowed, wanting to tell the world as he knew it about his discovery.

Eventually the rest of us went back to our cake. But not Tyler. He stood for half an hour staring at the moon. He cried when I took him inside and was only consoled when he realized that he could see the moon through his nursery window.

He awakened the next morning pointing at the window and looking for the moon. I tried to explain that it was gone, but he stared out his window calling, "Moon! Moon!" as if it were an animal he could coax back.

Finally, he looked at me and shrugged his little shoulders.

"No moon," he said sadly.

It was a small heartbreak, I knew, but I wanted desperately to explain it to him.

That night he returned to his window and began to call out to the object of his affections. But the moon had moved and now was seen only through the window in the living room. He squealed when he was reunited with his lost friend. And the next morning he jumped out of my arms and ran full speed to the living room to see if it was still there.

"No moon," he told me again sadly, after he had searched the sky.

Weeks passed, and then months. Every morning and every night Tyler looked out the windows searching for his friend. Most nights the moon didn't rise by the time he went to bed. When it did it was often covered by clouds. But Tyler never gave up. And although we tried to explain that the morning brought the sun, not the moon, Tyler was not impressed.

"No moon," he'd say, not with a sense of finality, but with stubborn hope that he would see it tomorrow.

Tyler's obsession had nearly become routine to us until one day in late fall. He had gone to the morning window on his usual mission. But instead of resignation, we heard squeals.

"Moon! Moon!" he yelled.

Surely he was mistaken, we thought. But we were wrong. On one side of the house the sun had risen. But on the other side, the moon still shone brightly, stubbornly defying its bedtime. And Tyler's face shone, too. He'd never given up, and his faith had been rewarded.

Sometimes the years open our eyes; sometimes they simply veil our sight. As I watched my son's face, I felt layers being peeled away. *How often do I see through a glass darkly simply because I lack faith?* I wondered. Once Tyler had seen the glorious moon, he had never again doubted its existence. It was beyond his comprehension, but not beyond his adoration. And even when it seemed to be absent for days, he never gave up hope.

My own faith in God paled in comparison. I could still remember seeing him for the first time and putting a name to my discovery. For a while I looked for him expectantly. Then the clouds came and the times of darkness, and I lost some of my initial fervor. Sure, I knew he was there. But I went about my business, taking care of problems and activities myself.

Seeing Tyler's devotion renewed my own faith. I began to expect to see God each and every day. Sometimes I barely caught a glimpse. Other days, it seemed that his light shone brightly throughout the day. Even on days when I hardly saw him at all, I kept looking. Now I realized that even when I didn't see him, he could see me. And I wanted him to know that this child was waiting expectantly, even stubbornly, no matter what anyone else might say.

13

From Power to Glory

T HE LAST THING IN THE WORLD I wanted to do was go to another formal dinner. The past months had been full of banquets and charity dinners, all important for one reason or another. Tonight was one more for one more reason I couldn't really remember. I was tired, getting a cold, and worse, I had to go alone because Tom was out of town and it was *my* friend that had brought on this invitation. Who would care if I didn't show up?

For some reason I couldn't decide whether to go or stay snug at home. It wasn't like me to vacillate on such an easy call. Then I began to realize that these nudges I had begun to feel lately came in different ways. Maybe this was one of them. Finally, I decided to pray.

"Keep me open, God," I began, as had become my custom. "Show me what you want me to do."

Less than an hour remained until the event. Without a clear sign, I decided to jump into the shower. If God called at least I wanted to have clean hair.

Coming out of the shower I began to sing a song I had heard on the radio earlier in the day. Almost without thinking, I dried my hair and put on my makeup. Then I laughed. I was feeling good, and I had a sudden burst of energy. God seemed to be propelling me toward the event.

Walking in at the end of the registration, I wandered through the crowd and saw only one person I knew. She was engaged in an animated conversation with two other men and didn't even notice my wave. The earlier fatigue returned. *Why had I bothered to come?* I thought. *Why am I putting myself through this?*

When the time came to be seated I realized that I had been placed at a table with guests of the honorees as well as those who had no particular affiliation. It was bad enough coming to a dinner I didn't want to attend, but being asked to sit with a table of extras seemed more than I could take.

"All right, God. If you're trying to teach me patience I'm working on it," I prayed, not very sweetly.

Finding my place, I made small talk with the others being seated at my table. Out of the corner of my eye I saw a man hovering nearby. He looked vaguely familiar, but I couldn't remember where I'd seen him. It wasn't unusual in Washington to see someone on the news and then later at the grocery store. This man was someone famous, but who? I saw others looking at him with more than a passing interest. And then I noticed how a few people made a special effort to steer a wide path around him, so as not to have to catch his eye or be caught in the same frame by one of the strolling photographers. *He was someone,* I thought. *Someone who has fallen from power.*

The man seemed to be used to this new treatment. He waited for others to approach him, but otherwise assumed a quiet, dignified pose. I watched him reach for the chair next to mine and sit down. As I saw his profile I realized who he was. A few years ago he had been one of the most powerful men in Washington, one of the men behind the president. He had regularly appeared on the front page of newspapers.

But then there had been charges of a conflict of interests. The president had quietly distanced himself from his former friend. There was talk of personal problems. And during a messy trial he was pictured in papers across the nation walking into the courthouse each day with a head bowed in embarrassment. Within a few months he moved from the White House to obscurity. And now he was about to sit down next to me. What in the world could I say to this man?

At first I considered pretending that I didn't know who he was. But I knew we'd run out of small talk and eventually move on to occupations. Perhaps I should just pretend I didn't know about his problems. But I would have had to have been locked in a closet for the past year to have missed the spectacle of his public trials.

Then I remembered something I'd read about him recently. It was a small piece in a newspaper I had seen when I was out of town. In it he'd talked openly about his political problems, his recovery from alcoholism, and some of the other personal problems that had plagued him. Perhaps he would be more open than I imagined.

He interrupted my thoughts by extending his hand and graciously introducing himself. I shook his hand, offered my name and said, "It's an honor to meet you, sir." I'm not sure where the words came from, but for some reason I wanted to give the man back some of the respect he seemed to have lost.

He smiled warmly. "Please, just call me Bill."

No one sat down on either side of us, so I had no choice but to chat with him. We talked for a few minutes about the weather, the program to come, the economy. Safe topics. Finally others filled in the table and the program began. I breathed a sigh of relief as dinner was served. Maybe I could get through the evening without having to really deal with Bill. Then a photographer approached our table. "Your picture is about to be taken," the voice next to me warned. He was giving me the chance to move away from him. Instead I leaned slightly toward him and smiled. It wasn't a particularly courageous move. I had little to lose in status or power. The flash went off, and the photographer moved on. Then Bill began to ask me questions, and I knew that we would be engaged in a conversation for awhile.

Finally I had to acknowledge that I knew who he was and what he'd gone through. I mentioned reading the article about him the week before.

"It was an interesting article," I observed, "but I

was confused by the ending. After detailing all you had gone through, the reporter ended with a quote saying that you'd never been happier. Was that quote inaccurate?"

"No," Bill said quietly, "that was absolutely correct."

"I don't mean to pry," I said, forgetting my earlier shyness, "but how could you be happier now than when you had so much power? Wouldn't you rather be sitting next to a prime minister than someone insignificant like me?"

Bill cleared his throat. "I don't talk about this a great deal in public, but since you asked I'll tell you. This might sound strange, but all the trouble I have been through was worth it because I found Jesus."

I laid my fork down on my plate and looked at him. His face was sincere, his tone of voice humble. I felt a sudden bond with him.

"No, that doesn't sound strange at all to me," I said softly. "My circumstances have been different, but I know exactly what you mean."

We talked then, not as people from two different worlds but as fellow pilgrims who had discovered a peace that passes understanding. He told me how his early interest in religion was replaced by the thrill of politics. He talked of making his political party his god and of enjoying the heady responsibilities that came from being so close to the president. He admitted how much he'd enjoyed knowing that people were afraid of him and that a word from him could make or break someone's career. He talked of it all with sadness, not

105

pride. With a sense of detachment. He described it "like Paul talking about Saul."

I listened and admitted to my own desire for control and power. And then I asked him why he hadn't been more public about his conversion.

"For years I used the media," he said. "I was good at it. But I don't want to use the media for Christ. I want to point people to him one by one. Besides, when Christ is working in your life it doesn't make good headlines. Who cares that I love the men in the shelter where I work more than I loved the power of the White House? It doesn't make sense to journalists. It only makes sense to those who have been there."

As the dinner came to a close I turned to him again.

"I didn't want to come here tonight," I said. "And when I saw you sitting down, I didn't know how I would ever carry on a conversation with you. But this has been a very moving experience for me. Thank you for telling me your story."

"God works in mysterious ways," he said with a grin. I noticed a man at another table looking at us with a puzzled expression. He was watching the man who had been considered the toughest politician in Washington sitting at a formal dinner, talking to a "nobody." I wanted to go to that man and say, "God changes people." But instead I hugged Bill good-bye and promised to pray for him. Most people in Washington think he has lost everything. Now I know better.

14

But For the Grace of God

I T WAS A PLEASANT DINNER, a chance to catch up with
an old friend I see every few months. When Liz
and I get together we tend to laugh uncontrollably
one minute and shed a few tears the next. She is one
of those rare friends with whom I feel equally comfortable sharing a meaningful Bible verse or a silly
joke.

And Liz is more than an accepting friend. She
challenges me to grow spiritually and reminds me of my
blessings when I become discouraged. She weeded
my flower garden with me once, just so we could
spend time together. She pushed me when I needed it
and held my hand when I couldn't even explain what I
was going through.

So that night when I asked, "What else is happening in your life?" I really wanted to know.

Liz looked at me for a moment, hesitated, and
then said, "I've decided to join a support group."

By the way she said it, I knew she had just handed
me a fragile truth.

I paused for a minute and then asked, "What type of group?"

Hesitantly she said, "One for women who have had abortions." There was an uncharacteristic silence between us as the full weight of her statement struck me.

"When did it happen?" I asked, hoping that I sounded more concerned than nosy.

"Several years ago, when I was still single," she said quietly. "I didn't really think I had any other option at the time. I knew it was wrong, but I didn't think I had a choice."

I had heard other women voice the same feelings, but they had always sounded like shallow excuses. But how could Liz—bright, sensitive Liz—say such things? How could these words come from my friend who loved God so much that she sometimes had tears in her eyes as she spoke of him? How could a woman I cared for say something I hated to hear?

The revelation didn't cause me to love Liz less; it just shook my security in what I thought I knew. *Women who have abortions aren't like me,* I had always believed. And yet I was confronted with the fact that a woman I loved, respected, and admired had done something that horrified me.

I left Liz that night with a hug, wanting her to know that I shared her sorrow over the act she committed so long ago and that I would help her through the recovery process. But I went home bewildered.

Finally, I began to pray and ask God to help me

understand how I could hate the sin and still love the sinner.

Slowly, gently, God seemed to whisper, "Yes, it could have been you." I wanted to protest my innocence, but I knew it was true. I was often selfish and expedient. There were times when I justified wrongs for "the greater good." And more shocking still, I could think that I was somehow above others who had given in to sins I would never commit. My "innocence" seemed suddenly legalistic. And Liz's revelation paled in comparison to what I began to see in my own life. I was horrified to see the pride I had in my definition of purity.

By the grace of God I had never been confronted with Liz's choice. Had I been, I pray that I would have made the right decision. But I will never know. How would I have dealt with the embarrassment I would have caused my family? With the guilt I would have felt? Would I have given the child up for adoption or tried to raise a baby on my own? How would I have told the people in my church? Would I have chosen the difficult path or taken the easy way out?

I began to weep then for Liz and all of the other women who had been confronted with the same decision. And I began to feel the weight of their pain. I no longer thought of women who had had abortions as different from me. I was one of them, just as surely as if I had made that awful decision myself.

The next week I attended my first pro-life rally. I did it not out of anger but out of sorrow for the babies lost and the women like Liz who had somehow felt that they had no choice. I joined the crowd not so much to change other people's minds but to say that I had changed my own. I stood there as a sinner, thanking God that in his mercy he had spared me. And I asked him to give me the courage to help other women, not because I was different but because I was very much the same.

15

Running in the Family

HURRYING AROUND AS USUAL, I bet myself I could make a quick trip to the supermarket. I ran in the door, grabbed a gallon of milk and a loaf of bread, and joined the customers in the express lane. I looked at my watch, proud of my efficiency. I'd be in and out of the grocery store in five minutes. Then I'd still have time to pick up the dry cleaning, order a picture frame, drop off the videotape, and pick up the kids at school.

My mental list-making was interrupted by a gurgling sound coming from the line to my right.

"Cute baby," I said to the woman who was patting the little bundle while trying to maneuver her cart into line.

"Thanks," she said barely squeezing out a smile. I took in the entire scene and began to understand her response. The baby was only weeks old. The cart over-flowed with staples and two sizes of diapers. In the seat a child who couldn't have been a year old was trying to launch herself at the rack of candy. And the woman looked like she'd passed exhaustion days before.

115

"It's not easy," I said empathetically, remembering the days of shopping with a newborn. But I'd never had it as hard as this woman. My first was done with bottles and diapers by the time my second came along.

"No, it's not," she said, looking as if she might cry. "But if I didn't do it we'd run out of everything."

"How are you going to get all this to the car?" I asked, by now identifying with her plight. She looked at me and just shook her head, overwhelmed by the next obstacle she would face.

I took another look at my watch and the quickly moving express line. Then I looked at her and her overflowing cart.

"Let me help you," I offered.

She started to protest, but then seemed unable to stop herself.

"Oh thank you," she said, a spark of life creeping back into her face.

I didn't make it to the dry cleaners after all. The videotape would cost another dollar. I added errands to my list for tomorrow with a sense of defeat. But despite my frustrations, I found myself smiling off and on for the rest of the day. *I really made a difference to that woman*, I thought. The cleaning and the video could wait. And then another thought occurred to me: *I need to thank Dad.*

I had learned the joy of being a Good Samaritan from my father. For as long as I could remember, Dad had gone out of his way to help others, to lend a hand, to share what he had. He never did it out of duty. He did it with joy and a sense of awe, that he was allowed to participate in the process of helping someone. And he taught his children to do the same, not as a discipline, but as a sacrament. From him we learned how blessed you are when you are allowed to help others.

There was no season when this lesson was more emphasized than Christmas. Every year we'd ask Dad what he wanted. And every year he'd say the same thing, "Don't buy me anything. Just give the money to people who really need it." He'd always get a little quiet when he said it, and we always knew that he was thinking about those who were less fortunate than our family. We'd still buy him presents, of course, but our Christmas season was always framed by his request at the beginning and his benediction at the end, "You shouldn't have bought so much for me. I have more than I will ever need." It was a gentle reminder in the midst of our present-opening frenzy. Receiving presents is nice. But giving to others feeds the soul.

Dad's example had made it easier for me to help other people. It's not because I'm less selfish than the next person. I have tasted the lasting joy of giving and learned that there is pleasure in the act. My instincts were shaped in the right direction from an early age. Being a Good Samaritan runs in our family.

As I look at my own boys, I know how much my attitudes are teaching them and shaping them whether I mean them to or not. They'll almost surely grow up to be list makers; they've watched their mother run through lists several times daily. But I hope they'll also

117

continue another tradition that runs in the family—
reaching out to others. More than that, I hope I will
make it easy for them to do the right thing. I want
them to know the sacred joy of giving before they
become too entangled in the fleeting pleasure of ac-
complishments. I want them to always know that
reaching beyond themselves will bring them a sense of
wholeness. I want them to understand that reaching
out to others makes it a little easier to reach out to
God.

It is not what we do that matters, but what a sovereign God chooses to do through us. God doesn't want our success; He wants us. He doesn't demand our achievements; He demands our obedience. The kingdom of God is a kingdom of paradox, where through the ugly defeat of a cross, a holy God is utterly glorified. Victory comes through defeat; healing through brokenness; finding self through losing self.

CHARLES COLSON
LOVING GOD

Those who live according to the sinful nature have their minds set on what that nature desires; but those who live in accordance with the Spirit have their minds set on what the Spirit desires.

ROMANS 8:5

Dear God,

I've done it again. Pulled back the reins. Taken back control. How I love to be in control.

Help me, God. I'm addicted to control. I want to trust you, but I act as if I still trust myself more. I know that I'm being foolish. Yet I can't help myself.

And I know that's the point: I *can't* help myself. Only you can help me. All I need to do is be willing to let you. I'm trying, God, I'm trying.

Thank you for encouraging me. For bothering with me. For surprising me. Thank you for caring about me, even when I care more about myself.

Help me to walk by faith, not by goals. Keep my eyes looking up and heart open. Remind me of the joy that comes from seeing your hand in my life.

I hand my life over once again . . .

16

Letting Go

M OMMY, I DID IT!" CHASE yelled as he burst through the front door.

I leaned over the upstairs railing and saw his beaming face and tousled hair.

"I rode my bike all by myself," he announced, gasping excitedly. "Come watch."

I dropped what I was doing and ran down the stairs and out to the front porch. While his father stood on the sidewalk, Chase climbed on his bike and began peddling. He wobbled from side to side and then, just as he seemed about to fall, he took off down the street, the picture of confidence. For a split second he took his eyes off the sidewalk ahead and flashed me a big smile.

"See!" he said triumphantly.

Tom and I clapped and cheered his success.

"You did it!" we yelled, thrilled that our son had conquered this obstacle.

The victory had been hard earned. For months he had been frustrated in his attempts to conquer the two-wheeler. Time after time I would run down the street stooped over as I held on to the back of his bicycle seat.

"Don't let go!" he'd remind me nervously.

And then, after one more unsuccessful day, he'd drag his bike home dejectedly and announce, "I'm the only kid in the whole world who can't ride a two-wheeler."

I understood his feelings. I still remember the day that all my friends took off down the street on their shiny bicycles, and I was too ashamed to bring out mine because it had training wheels. And I remember the sweet victory of conquering that bicycle and sailing down the block for the first time. I wanted that sense of freedom for Chase, and yet I was sad to realize that he'd never again say, "Don't let go."

It's a tricky business, this holding on and letting go. I have yet to find its rhythm. But in my nearly seven years of parenting I have discovered that the holding on is the easy part. It's the letting go that fills me with dread and self-doubt. What if I let go too soon? But part of me fears that I won't let go at all, stifling the child who needs to grow into a man.

"Yes, you can sleep over at Peter's house," I say, proud of myself for opening this door for my son. But then the doubts begin to roll in like waves, and I can hardly catch my breath. What if the boys begin to wrestle on the bunk beds and Chase falls off? What about the creek behind Peter's house? What if . . . ? I take a deep breath and fight my urge to hold on to my son. Instead I do what has become a daily habit. I pray for guardian angels to surround him and protect him. And then I ask for peace and wisdom. Clinging is not the answer, I know, but I need divine help to unclench my grip.

I am ashamed to admit how little I prayed before I had children. I was gliding through life, occasionally offering thanks or requesting a favor. Now prayer is all I have when I feel the need to hold on but see the importance of letting go. Prayers go with my children when I'm not there. I take comfort in imagining God's open palms beneath my children as they climb, his gentle touch easing them away from danger, his steady hand guiding them as they ride down the street. When I can't—or shouldn't—hold on I ask him to be there for me. Some days it is all that keeps my mother love from smothering the flicker of independence that deserves to be fanned.

On one hand, I am surprised that letting go is so hard for me. I have always been an independent person who ran from suffocating friendships and expected routines. I understand this need my children have to test their wings. And yet the mother in me recognizes the vulnerability inherent in independence, the headiness of freedom that can scoff at caution. I have so little control as a mother. It is the lesson God is teaching me over and over again.

As I tuck Chase into bed he says, with six-year-old bravado, "Riding my bike was easy, Mom."

I smile as I think about the number of times I went to bed with backaches, the many times the training wheels came off only to be put back on.

"Yes, it is easy once you know what to do," I agree.

Leaning over to me conspiratorially, he drops his voice.

"You want to know my secret?"

I nod, waiting.

"I just pretended that Daddy was still holding on to the back of my bike, and then I wasn't scared. That's how I learned to ride all by myself."

I hug my son and marvel at his words. And just for a moment I think I feel a gentle hand on my shoulder, steadying me as I stumble along this path of motherhood.

"Trust me," he seems to whisper. I take a deep breath and try to let go.

17

Mom, Am I a Christian?

C HASE, EAT YOUR CHEERIOS," I said, exasperated as I watched my son dawdle over his breakfast. His spoon was poised halfway between the cereal bowl and his mouth as big drops of milk plopped back onto the table.

"Chase!" I repeated a moment later. "You're going to be late for school." But Chase sat mesmerized, listening to a tape that played background music to the breakfast noise.

Lately nothing seemed to get through to my son. I had to remind him over and over to do such basic things as get dressed, brush his teeth, put on his seat belt. I hated nagging him, but in the past month he'd changed from a cheerful, cooperative child into an independent, absent-minded dawdler. Where was his mind these days?

I watched as Chase put the spoon back into his cereal and stirred it around and around.

"Chase!" I said harshly. "Eat!"

"Mom," he said casually, oblivious to my tirade. "Am I a Christian?"

133

"What?" His question caught me off guard. Then I realized that the children's tape he had been listening to talked about who a Christian was. "You are if you ask Jesus to come live in your heart," I responded almost automatically. "Would you like to do that?"

"Yes, Mom," Chase said without hesitation. "But I think I need privacy."

Once again I was taken aback by his response. We had just discussed the idea that people needed privacy when they changed their clothes or did something personal. The fact that Chase felt he needed privacy for this decision made me think he had some idea of its significance.

"You're right," I agreed. "This is very important and very personal."

"Okay," he said cheerfully. "I'll do it later."

He's so young, I reminded myself. *Don't push him.* I couldn't imagine how this spacey child could suddenly focus on such a significant decision.

Gulping down his breakfast, Chase jumped up, kissed me, and ran to the front door to await his ride, leaving me to ponder what had just happened. I replayed the tape he had been listening to. There, very clearly, was the message that being a Christian wasn't just being good. It meant making a commitment. And Chase was very good about commitments. If he promised to do something, he always followed through.

That night, as Chase got ready for bed, I asked, "Would you like your prayer to be special tonight?"

"Yes," Chase said. "I want to ask Jesus to live in my heart." After a day of school and playing with friends, he still remembered that morning's decision. "What do I do?"

"You can just talk to Jesus like you usually do," I explained. "But this time ask him to forgive your sins and live in your heart forever."

"Okay," he said. "Dear Jesus, please forgive me and come live in my heart—oops, excuse me, Jesus."

Opening his eyes, Chase looked at me.

"Mom, will Jesus really live inside my heart forever and ever?"

"Yes, honey," I assured him.

"I'm back, Jesus," he said, closing his eyes. "And please come live in my heart forever and ever and ever. Amen."

I hugged my son and prayed that Jesus would help this simple prayer be meaningful in his life. Then Chase went over to the calendar on his wall and drew a big heart on the date.

"So we remember that this is the day Jesus came into my heart," he explained.

After I tucked my son in and turned off the lights, I sat on the stairs and wondered again if he really understood the commitment he had just made. And then, for some reason, I began to review my life. I remembered the night I had asked Jesus to come into my heart. And I remembered how many times I had kept him out of my life, too. I saw how little I had understood about the enormity of my own commitment along the way. I realized that each day brought me challenges that would have been too much for me to tackle in the past. But somehow, God had given me what I needed to move on. When I trusted him with childlike faith, I was fine. But when I tried to figure things out on my own, I stumbled.

"Thank you, Lord," I prayed, "for reminding me of the importance of having faith like a child's. Please teach my son gently, and remind him to hold your hand. Amen."

18

In Faith, Believing...

I FOUND IT!" CHASE YELLED, displaying the once-missing toy for his friend's inspection.

"How did you find it?" Sam asked. "We've been looking for an hour."

"I just prayed, and when I looked down, it was right there," Chase declared.

"Wow," Sam said in awe. "You mean you just pray and then you can find things?"

"Sure," Chase said with great confidence.

I stood in the kitchen, listening to the children's theological discussion. On one hand, I was pleased by Chase's openness to God and his sincere belief in prayer. But I wondered if I should set the record straight before he was disappointed by a prayer that *wasn't* answered. Something told me to wait. God had so often taught me lessons through Chase. Maybe I should look for the lesson instead of trying to teach one . . .

A week later I was driving down a freeway in Los Angeles, late for my flight that would take me home after a business trip. My rental car's gas gauge was dangerously close to empty, but I didn't have time to stop for a fill up. Then I came around a bend into a sea of red brake lights. The freeway was hopelessly backed up. I sat in bumper to bumper traffic, watching the needle move further to the left.

The slowed traffic gave me plenty of time to look around at the neighborhood through which the freeway passed. It was a former industrial area that looked gutted. Buildings were empty. Windows broken, walls spray painted with gang symbols. No gas stations in sight.

I crept nearer to an exit, but decided I was better off on the freeway. I could go for blocks looking for a gas station in that neighborhood. And what would happen if I ran out of gas there? I shivered at the thought.

The traffic jam seemed endless.

"Please God," I began to pray, "don't let me run out of gas."

Another exit appeared ahead, but the neighborhood didn't look any better.

And then I saw it. A bright orange sign just to the left of the exit ramp promised "Gas for less." I inched up to the exit, sneaking a quick look at the gas gauge which had come to rest at the end of the red zone.

"Just one more block," I prayed.

I pulled into the gas station and for a moment feared that it was closed. Then an attendant stuck his head out the door of the station and looked at me strangely. He looked around, then walked quickly over to my car.

"Where are you from?" he asked, clearly surprised to see a woman in a business suit.

"The East Coast," I said.

The man just shook his head, obviously thinking I was out of my mind to venture into this part of town.

He filled up my car and came back to my window. "You keep your door locked," he said. "And you better get right back on that freeway," he added, pointing me in the direction of the entrance ramp.

I thanked him, and drove away, looking around at the burned out buildings and tough-looking young men who stood in a group on one of the corners.

"Thank you, God," I prayed in relief.

I was back on the freeway before I really relaxed. *I could have been killed*, I realized with new intensity. *How stupid it was to let my gas tank get so low*, I added. And then I began to wonder about my prayer. Was it any different than Chase's? Did I pray and the gas station appeared in the middle of nowhere? Did God just save my life?

For as much as I had learned about God, I still approached him like a spoiled child. "Get me out of this trouble," was my most common theme.

I was still pondering my shameful approach to prayer when I opened up Oswald Chamber's classic, *My Utmost for His Highest.* "'Your father knows what you need before you ask,'" he explained. "The point of asking is that you may get to know God better."

141

I thought about Chase talking to God about his lost toy. His sincere belief and open heart weren't signs of naivete. He believed God would help him and he had. It suddenly occurred to me that God must get great pleasure from Chase's trust.

My trust came more encumbered by doubts and pragmatism. It was tarnished by years of believing more in myself than in God's ability to help me. It was handed over grudgingly, often after I had tried to tap my own abilities and found them lacking.

And yet God had answered my prayer just as he had answered Chase's. He was as willing to give to me as he was to my son who loved him with childish openness. He was the same God for both of us. But one of us still had a lot to learn.

19

Fear Not, But Behold...

I DON'T RIDE THE SUBWAY VERY OFTEN. But my meeting was in the heart of downtown and instead of searching for a parking garage, I decided to take the Metro. As I stood waiting for the train, I looked at the people gathering on the platform. A well-dressed businessman, an elderly couple, and a young woman waited with me. The train roared to a stop, the doors whooshed open, and I stepped on and sat down in a nearly empty car.

I pulled out some reading material and became engrossed as the train sped along, stopping at points along the way into town. I was interrupted by someone sitting down next to me.

"Excuse me," he said as he bumped my arm.

He was young, maybe sixteen, but he was very tall and muscular. His shoes were the latest style, his running suit flashy. He wore a gold chain around his neck and an oversized ring on his finger. *Why isn't he in school?* I wondered.

I took a quick look around the train. The car was still only half full. *Why had this young man decided to sit next to me when he could have sat alone?* I thought nervously.

"You look like you're in business," the young man said in a friendly tone. Too friendly.

I looked at him sideways.

"Yes, I am," I responded.

Why was he talking to me? People didn't talk to each other on the subway—unless they wanted something.

You're overreacting, part of my mind scolded. All young black men aren't criminals. Then I thought of the article I had just read in the newspaper. "Chances are, you will be a victim of crime sometime in your life," the article concluded. *Was this my time?* I wondered.

"What are you reading?" the young man asked.

"Help me, God," I prayed. "I don't want to make him angry. I need wisdom."

"It's just a business magazine," I said. "Would you like to look at it?" I offered.

He seemed genuinely pleased. "Thanks," he said, taking the magazine and beginning to page through it.

I pretended to read another magazine, but all the time I was thinking. My stop was coming up. If I was the only one getting off, I'd stay on the train, I decided. I looked around the car for someone who might be able to help me if I needed it. No one looked very strong—or helpful.

"Do you know if I need to transfer at Metro Center to get to the airport?" the man asked.

"Yes, you do," I said, knowing then that he would be getting off at my stop. I'd be late for my meeting if I went to the stop beyond that one and then returned. But my life might be in danger if I got off with this young man. I decided to wait.

The stop was approaching as he began to stand up. I breathed a sigh of relief. Then he sat down again and looked at me.

"Thanks for being so kind," he said.

"What?" I said, startled.

"I just wanted to thank you for being kind to me," he said. "See I'm a Christian, and I know that doing things right and being good to people is important. But I also know that you don't always get rewarded for it. So I just want you to know that I appreciate it."

I stuttered out a thank you as he stood again and then walked into the crowd. I jumped up and hurried off the train. The young man was far ahead of me as he stepped off the platform and out into the street. "Wait," I wanted to call out to the man I had been afraid of just moments before. "You've made a mistake," I wanted to say. But I didn't know how I'd explain that my kindness had come less from Christian love than from fear and self-defense. I wanted to confess that I had thought the worst of him, but he disappeared around the corner as I got caught up in the crowd.

Wisdom. I had prayed for wisdom, I realized. God had honored my prayer without my realizing it. My knowledge wasn't deep enough to see beyond the dress of the young man. But God knew his heart. And he knew mine, too.

"I'm sorry," I prayed. "Take away the bigotry that I can't even see. Help me to be less concerned about myself and more concerned about others. And give me eyes to see your angels."

20

Down to Earth

T HE SUN WAS STREAMING through the skylight of the restaurant, surrounding Anne Ortlund in an ethereal glow. I had come to interview her for a magazine article, but as my tape recorder whirred, my mind was less on reporting than on applying Anne's words in my own life.

A unique party had just been held in Anne's honor. The guests were all women who had become Christians or grown in their faith as a result of Anne. For twenty years she had been working with small groups of women, teaching them the Bible and the basics of Christian living. After a year, each of these women was challenged to go out and teach others. And they had. Four "generations" of women—more than six hundred individuals—had been directly or indirectly affected by Anne's life.

I've always admired Anne. Her writing has in-spired me; her speaking has taught me. But what I like best about her is that she is a real person. She has real-people faults that she openly admits are only under control through God's grace.

151

"I talk too much," she once admitted. "But God has made progress with me. I can see it," she said, as if she were referring to someone else.

Anne began to tell me about the women in her groups, some of whom had turned to God in times of despair, others who had turned their backs on wealth and status in order to pursue God's plan for their lives. As I listened I found myself yearning for the growth Anne talked about; the ability to follow God boldly.

"Oh Anne, I wish I lived near you so I could join one of your groups and grow too," I said. I felt such a need to begin to work out spiritually, to develop my faith, and to build spiritual stamina. I could relate to someone like Anne, who didn't act like she had been born on a spiritual plane. If I could only find someone like her to help me grow.

"The best way to grow in your faith is to teach others," Anne said. As I looked at her quizzically she challenged me directly: "Start a group yourself."

"Oh, but I couldn't," I blurted out. How could I explain that my faith had been shallow for so many years, that my knowledge of God was still at a pre-school level? How could I confess my inadequacies? How could I tell her that I was starting from scratch myself, having demolished a shaky structure and now having little more than a foundation?

Anne seemed to sense my struggle, but she didn't back down.

"Even if you only know one verse, teach that to someone else. Then go back and learn something to teach the next week. You'll have to work to keep ahead of your students. And that's the best way to learn," she said.

Our interview time was over, but Anne's words continued to play in my mind.

"Oh, God, I couldn't," I finally said in prayer. But I knew enough to ask him to show me the way. "I'm too afraid to try something like this. I don't even know where to begin."

The next week my friend Becky called.

"I haven't been involved in a Bible study for awhile," she said. "Would you like to start one with me?"

"I can't believe you're saying this!" I responded. I told her about Anne's challenge and my prayer. Becky knew how to lead Bible studies. All she wanted me to do was provide a location and help lead the discussion times. I felt fine about providing the place, but I still worried about leading the discussion. Still, God seemed to be propelling the events forward.

"Okay," I prayed, "I'll hold on for the ride."

"Who should we invite?" I asked, my insecurities again overtaking me. What if people came expecting me to have all the answers, what if they wanted more of me than I could give, what if . . .

"Let's pray about it," Becky said matter-of-factly.

"Of course," I responded, wishing I had thought of that.

The next week a business associate came to me hesitantly.

153

"I know you have Bibles around your office," she said. "My kids are studying things in school about the Bible, and I wonder if you have a book I could read to learn what the Bible is all about. I went to church as a kid, but I really didn't learn much."

I took a deep breath.

"Sure, I can get you some books," I said. "We're also starting a Bible study at my house soon. Would you like to come?"

I waited for her to back off, but instead she responded as if I'd invited her to dinner.

"That sounds great. I'd love to," she said. I stood there for a minute stunned by her response.

That afternoon an old friend called.

"You know, we haven't been very good about going to church," she said. "But I've been thinking that I really want to get back on track spiritually."

With growing confidence, I told her about the developing Bible study.

"Great!" she said. "That's exactly what I was looking for."

Over the next weeks Becky had similar reactions from friends. Soon we had a group of seven women who were enthusiastic about coming to my house every Monday night to study the Bible. My husband promised to put the kids to bed and to do whatever he could to get the house ready for the group. Almost without my involvement, God had orchestrated everything.

Just as Anne had promised, I had to work hard to keep ahead of the others, even though few of them

had a church background. We studied the Gospel of
John together, a book I thought might be too elemen-
tary at first and later discovered had more nuances
than I had imagined.

Working through the chapters, we learned about
Jesus. At first some of the women were skeptical. Then
one night the greatest cynic of all in the group proclaimed, "I'm really beginning to like this guy Jesus."
As the weeks passed we learned more about each
others' lives and how this Bible study was beginning
to influence entire families.

Then Becky had to leave town one week, and she
asked me to lead the study. All of my self-doubt
flooded back in. Week after week she had done an
incredible job of leading the group while I had listened
and helped as best I could. But me *lead* the study? I'd
be humiliated.

"Help me God," I prayed when it was clear that I
could not plead my way out of this role.

I studied for hours all week in preparation, but as
the women filed into my home, I still felt unprepared.

"Let them look at you, not me," I prayed to God.

All of the women volunteered answers and par-
ticipated in the discussion as if to help me out. The
hour passed quickly, and I breathed a sigh of relief as
we ended. I had made it through somehow.

As one of the women left, she stopped for a
minute. "I know you said that it wasn't easy for you to
lead this group," she said, "but I want you to know
that your style of leadership really appeals to me.

You're so down-to-earth that I feel like I can relate to what you're saying. I didn't feel too intimidated to speak out tonight."

I thanked her for her encouragement, closed the door, and began to relax. And then I laughed. *What a sense of humor God has,* I thought to myself. The very quality I had admired in Anne was what someone else had seen in me. "When I am weak, then I am strong," the Apostle Paul said. The words took on new meaning as I cleared the coffee cups away and cleaned up the living room.

"Thank you, God," I prayed, "for working through me, even when I was afraid. Help me to be brave enough to let you take me where I need to go."

21

God's Fool

I SLAMMED THE PHONE DOWN hard enough to earn a disapproving frown from the person at the next pay phone. Just then the announcement came that my plane was about to depart.

"Wait!" I yelled to the flight attendant about to close the door on the jetway.

As I handed her my ticket and sprinted on board, my stomach was churning. The last thing I needed right now was a major disruption. I had planned to use my flying time to put the last touches on my speech for a women's conference. I wanted it to be good, to be effective. Speaking was never easy for me, and I needed all of the preparation time I could get. But now all I could think about was the conversation I had just had.

As the airplane lifted off I began to ask myself how this could have happened. How could an agreement I thought was clear be denied by this man? I was angry, hurt, disappointed. *Where had I gone wrong?* I wondered. I sifted through conversations and agreements, implications and reprisals. I thought

of all the times I had warned the man that the changes
he wanted to make to his brochure would be costly.
"I'll pay for them," he'd said. "Just do it quickly." I
ended with one conclusion: My greatest mistake had
been to trust the man.

"What a fool I've been," I thought to myself.

Realizing I had been a fool was one thing; continu-
ing to be one was another. I pulled out my pad on which
I had intended to make notes for my speech. Instead, I
began to make a list of people to call and information to
gather for my counterattack. I wasn't going to take this
lying down! At the top of my list was my attorney.

As soon as my plane landed I called him and, as
calmly as possible, recited the details of the situation.

"There wasn't time, so I never revised the contract
to account for all the changes," I admitted, knowing
how naive I must sound to my attorney who spent his
days working out complex agreements.

"You do have a new contract," he said. "It simply
isn't in writing." I breathed a sigh of relief. The law
was on my side.

Then I called a friend who knew all the extra work
I had gone through to complete the job on time.

"How could he do such a thing!" she cried out
over the phone, confirming my feelings. She reassured
me, consoled me, and shared my anger. I felt vindi-
cated.

By now hours had ticked by. I was calmer about
the business situation, but my speech was still rough. I
pulled out my notes and began frantically assembling

the pieces of my message. I was speaking to a group of women about knowing God's will. It was an important message. It had to be just right.

I began to read the words I had written. "Most of the time we start with what we want to do, then we ask God to bless it. Instead we need to ask God to show us the way, even if it's not where we want to go." They were my words, in my handwriting, but I looked at them as if I were seeing them for the first time. I believed those words. I try to live by them. And I had denied them all day.

I shuddered as I thought of the events of the last few hours. I had gone from anger to action without ever uttering a word of prayer. In frustration I had turned to my attorney, not to God.

Putting my speech notes aside, I tried to pray.

"I'm still angry, God," I admitted. "You know it and I know it. I feel wronged and hurt. I haven't asked what you want me to do. I'm not sure I really want to know. I'm not ready to give up my anger or to give up control. Help me want to do your will." It was the best I could do; the most honest I could be. I felt as though my hands were still clenched, ready for a fight. But I had at least offered my fists up to God.

I noticed the time. Half an hour left until I was to speak. Grabbing my notes back, I continued to read. "Therefore do not be foolish, but understand what the Lord's will is."

Foolish. What a word! That's exactly how I felt. I had trusted the man and I felt foolish. But I was finally

beginning to see that I would be a greater fool if I
ignored God.

"Okay, God," I prayed. "I may not like it, but I
will try to do your will. Show me what you want me
to do."

I read through more of my speech and then
stopped, stunned by another verse I had noted: "For
the foolishness of God is wiser than man's wisdom,
and the weakness of God is stronger than man's
strength." I knew this verse by heart. How had I been
able to ignore the words all day?

I felt tears forming in my eyes as understanding
flooded in. "Oh, God, you want me to be a fool, don't
you?" As I prayed, I began to feel a release from the
anger that had gripped me. The incongruity of what
was happening made me shake my head. I had always
prided myself in my ability to do business wisely. I
hated to be taken advantage of. It seemed so unjust.
But I could see now that justice wasn't the issue at all.
Pride was. "You know how hard this is for me, don't
you, God? You know how hard it is for me to be taken
for a fool."

To choose the role of a fool was unthinkable. And
yet what if I accepted the situation without a fight?
What if I allowed God to do what he wanted, not what
I wanted? What if I allowed the man to "win"? What if
I lost the money I had spent? It would be difficult for
me; the very opposite of my inclinations. But I would
do it knowing that I was being God's fool. I felt surprisingly peaceful at the thought. And suddenly wise.

Only God could change me in such a dramatic way. Only God would care enough to try.

I stood before the group of women that night without the fear I usually experienced when I spoke. I told them a simple story about pride and foolishness. And then I told them about the miracle of change.

Nothing is more surprising than the rise of the new within ourselves. We do not foresee or observe its growth. We do not try to produce it by the strength of our will, by the power of our emotion, or by the clarity of our intellect. . . . The new being is born in us, just when we least believe in it. It appears in the remote corners of our souls which we have neglected for a long time.

PAUL TILLICH

THE SHAKING OF FOUNDATIONS

"One thing I do know. I was blind but now I see."

JOHN 9:25

Dear God,

I know you've been preparing me as much as I would let you. But I'm not any more ready today than I have been in the past. These ups and downs are too much.

People have seen you in me so they come for answers. I don't have any, God. I don't know how to make sense of these events that turn lives upside down and leave them in shambles.

I know you are there. And I know I can trust you. But I wonder when you will show me what you are about. When will you help me understand?

I have learned so much, but I know so little. Sometimes I look back and see the path I have come along. We have come a long way together. But I still can't see the path ahead. Yet I am finally convinced—most of the time—that I don't want to or need to see the future. It's enough to know you are there lighting the path.

Life isn't random, and the path doesn't lead to nowhere. I know that now. But knowing is worse, in a way, and the very opposite of what I once thought. You have shown me that there is joy in pain, wisdom in foolishness, strength in weakness. And most of all that there's no making sense of any of it by myself.

Oh God, I need you so. Without you I think I have the answers. And I forget to even ask the questions.

22

Jesus Is Coming

A GENTLE BREEZE WAS BLOWING off the ocean, picking up a few grains of sand from Chase's drying sandcastle.

"Be careful so you don't get sand on anyone," I reminded my son, aware that the beach was so overcrowded that personal space was at a minimum.

My older son and I were enjoying an afternoon together while Dad stayed back at the hotel with baby brother. I wanted to be sure that Chase got personal attention on this vacation, since his life with us was now shared with a sibling. And with Chase in school all day now, it seemed like I hardly had any time with my little boy.

Children squealed and splashed in the surf as Chase ran down to fill up his bucket with more water for his building project. A dozen radios all seemed tuned to different stations. Bright beach towels, covering every inch of sand, were occupied by every imaginable size, shape, and color of person. Even the sky was cluttered with kites and buzzing planes that flew over the beach, trailing advertising banners for suntan lotion and happy hours.

Chase and I had carefully constructed our personal oasis earlier in the day. Now it seemed under siege by rowdy teenagers on one side and a family that kept adding newcomers on the other. Slowly but surely our piece of beach was being invaded by coolers and beach chairs. Feeling claustrophobic, I laid back and closed my eyes for a moment to block out the overwhelming scene.

"Mom, Mom!" I heard Chase yell, and I jumped up, fearing that a wave was engulfing him. My heart was racing as I looked around, trying to spot his familiar red swimsuit among all of the colors on the beach. I relaxed a bit as I realized that he was still just a few feet away from me, within my reach. He looked at me with excitement, not fear.

"Mom! Jesus is coming!" he yelled over the blasting of the radio.

Confused, I looked around again, this time trying to see whom he might be looking at. The scene hadn't changed. The stomach of the man next to me seemed to have grown brighter red. A teenage girl stretched seductively for her boyfriend. A baby wailed and shook his empty bottle. The family to our left had added two more people and pushed their chairs right up to our towel.

I looked back to Chase and saw his face glowing as he looked up into the sky.

"There, Mom. See?" he exclaimed.

I looked up, wondering, just wondering for a moment . . .

And then I heard the familiar buzz of the engine and saw the trailing banner. JESUS IS COMING it proclaimed. Chase turned back to me, his face still glowing.

"See Mom? I read it all by myself."

I tousled the sandy hair of my budding reader. Ever since Chase had learned to read in school he had delighted in surprising me by sounding out signs and instructions. But this time his thrill went beyond his pride in being able to read the sign.

"Where is he, Mom?" Chase asked, taking the banner literally.

"I think he's probably still in heaven, honey," I answered gently. I had always been amazed by Chase's open heart. Now I realized that he was genuinely thrilled at the thought of Jesus coming. "That sign just means that he's coming someday."

"Oh," Chase said, disappointed. "So when is he coming, Mom?" he asked with anticipation.

I searched my mind for a biblical answer to his practical question. And then I remembered the carefully memorized verse: ". . . when we least expect it," I answered, looking around at the gaudy beach scene. Surely there couldn't be a less likely place for the Son of God to come again. Would anyone even notice if he appeared on this beach today? Would anyone turn off their radio or stop jogging along the surf? I looked at the faces of the people. Were there any people here who wanted Jesus to come into their world?

"I guess we better be ready," Chase said, going back to his building and making me wonder how much he understood about Jesus' coming. And then I wondered how Jesus felt as he looked upon this scene. He must be pleased by the enthusiastic response of this little boy. But what about the rest of the people, so caught up in their own world?

And then I thought about my own life and the way Jesus had come when I least expected it. I had been caught up in my own pursuits, going about my own business. I don't know when I fell out of love with my heavenly Father. I remember having a child-like faith that gave way to an intellectual understanding. Then I simply got caught up in the stuff of life. My faith became an accessory, not a way of living. I asked God in as a guest, never allowing him to overstay his visit.

But when I ran out of faith in myself, Jesus had come to replace clichés with heartfelt prayers, and piety with passion. He had shaken me out of comfort and replaced it with joy. His coming in my life had been as significant as if he had appeared suddenly on this beach.

I leaned over toward my son.

"You know what, Chase? If we let him, Jesus will come every day."

"Right here, Mom?" Chase asked, looking around.

"No, honey, right here," I said, pointing to his heart.

"I know that, Mom," Chase said smiling at me.

And as he went back to building his sandcastle he began to sing, "Jesus loves me, this I know . . ."

I sat in the middle of the same crowded beach, but somehow the radios seemed less assaulting and the people more attractive.

". . . little ones to him belong," Chase sang, and I silently thanked God for my son's open heart.

"Help me to have the heart of a child and the openness to you," I prayed.

And then, before I laid back down on my beach towel, I looked around just one more time. Wondering, just wondering . . .

23

Promises to Keep

W HENEVER I THINK OF ISABEL—and I think of her often—I see the same expression. It didn't matter if she was dressed for a formal occasion or wearing blue jeans. Her face was always the same: eyes wide open, lips slightly parted, she seemed about to discover something new. It was not so much a look of surprise as an expression that seemed to invite. "Surprise me!"

Her children enjoyed doing just that. I think of her squealing with delight as her oldest son presented her with a worm. She wasn't one of those "not now" mothers. Instead, she jumped right into her children's games, understanding them from a child's point of view. One day she spent several minutes explaining to me exactly who was a good guy and who was a bad guy in the world of G.I. Joes. She had obviously spent many hours in "combat" herself.

Isabel's childlike quality took many forms. At a party she was the one who told stories and got everyone laughing. But she was also the one who noticed

the person who seemed to be left out. She managed to
make everyone feel important with her genuine, guile-
less interest.

Isabel always saw the intrinsic humor in life, even
when she faced the news that cancer had invaded her
lively body.

"Are you angry?" I asked her.

"Yes," she replied. "I'm angry that I wasted so
many hours in advanced aerobics classes."

We both laughed, but later I cried. It was unthinkable that anything could slow Isabel down.

The chemotherapy was only a temporary setback
for my energetic friend. Once the initial waves of
nausea passed, she was back to her regular schedule—
including the aerobics classes. It was her way of saying
that she refused to give cancer control over her life.

"I'm going to be one of those percentages that
prove the experts wrong," she'd say. And some days
she'd add, "I've got to be. I've got three kids to raise."
It was that postscript that said it all. She wasn't fighting for her own life.

One day, less than a year after the initial diagnosis
and with the news that the cancer had spread, Isabel and
I talked.

"I'm scared," she said. "Not for myself, but for my
kids. What will happen to them?"

Even then I refused to believe the worst.

A week later, her fear had turned to pragmatism.
She was in so much pain that the doctor wanted to
increase her medication, but she refused, knowing that

the relief would also dull her mind. She was determined to be there for others as long as she could.

"What can I do?" I asked her.

"I haven't had a chance to get Stephen new pajamas," she said in a voice distorted with pain. "He likes the ones that are all cotton."

I promised to get the pajamas, not knowing that it was the last conversation I would have with my friend.

A few days later, after the funeral, I delivered the pajamas to little Stephen.

"Your mommy loved you so much that she wanted to be sure you had the right kind of pajamas," I told him. I looked at his face and noticed the expression for the first time. "You look a lot like your mother," I said.

"I know," he said, smiling.

I think of Isabel too often these days to have pure motives. Yes, I miss her. But it has been nearly two months since I sobbed through her funeral, and even then I knew that I was crying as much for me as I was for her.

Sometimes at night, when I am surrounded by the rhythmic breathing of my family, I think of Isabel and I cry. I have stopped asking God why he took her. I doubt that I will ever understand. But I do understand something clearly now: Even women with children to raise sometimes die. Women like Isabel. Women like me.

I think of our last conversation and I know that I would have had the same concerns as Isabel.

"I don't want anything more for me," she told me. "I just want to live to take care of my children."

To buy them cotton pajamas. To cut their sandwiches on the diagonal. To be sure their hair is parted on the right side. I know these worries. *Who would care if I were gone?*

This morning I spent extra time snuggling in bed with my youngest. Last night I repacked my older son's lunch twice, just to be sure it contained all of his favorites. I did these things for my boys and for myself and for Isabel.

I have a picture in my mind of Isabel balancing her youngest on her hip while she straightened her little girl's hair and carried on a conversation with me. When her older son bounded up to her with his discovery, she didn't say "not now." "Oh look," she gasped with joy.

I learned a great deal from my friend Isabel. I learned to laugh a little more, to greet surprises with enthusiasm, and to watch out for those who need a friend. But mostly I learned that a mother can't afford to say, "Not now."

24

Perspective

I T IS THE MIDDLE OF THE MORNING and I am stuck in a traffic jam. What should have been a ten-minute trip from one appointment to the next is threatening to stretch the twenty-minute mark. *What could be tangling a major street at 10:30 in the morning?* I wonder.

And then I notice the hearse coming slowly toward me. I note it without much interest. Could a funeral procession be holding up traffic? Frustrated, I look at the line of cars following the black Cadillac. A gleaming Jaguar creeps slowly along and then stops even with my car. I try not to stare at the red-eyed driver. He is young—not yet forty I guess—and well dressed. The next car is a BMW, and the inhabitants are two young couples. They are followed by more sports and luxury cars, all driven by well-dressed young men and a few women, their mouths set in grim resolve.

A friend of theirs has died, I surmise. Perhaps a man like them—young and successful. The look I see on their faces is a combination of shock and denial: Young successful men don't die, they all seem to say.

I feel their shock; I absorb their pain. Suddenly the traffic jam and my appointment seem unimportant. My own friend, my bright, vivacious, wacky friend has died, too. A horn honks behind me. I cannot see ahead because of the tears blinding my vision. Pulling over to the side of the road, I begin to sob uncontrollably for the young man who died, for Isabel and her children, and for myself.

I have come so far, but not far enough. I still do not have any understanding of who must die or why it must happen. But now when I cry, I cry out to God. *Please give me some perspective*, I beg.

Perspective. It's one of the attributes God embodies and mortals covet. Perspective comes to us too late, long after we have asked *why* a thousand times and offered puny theories in a vain hope that we will somehow hit upon the right answer, as if it were a game of chance. The Bible says that we see through a glass darkly. But I'm afraid this is wishful thinking. We don't see through the glass at all most days. We rarely even look in the right direction. We squint and stare as if we have some idea of what we are looking for, as if it is somehow in our power to will context onto our haphazard lives.

In fact, we have nothing to be proud of when we truly gain perspective. It is an example of grace, unearned and undeserved. It is as if God finally feels sorry for us, wallowing around in our silly theories.

And so he reaches down, takes us by the shoulders, and turns us slowly and gently in the right direction. Then, even then, few of us see it at all. He must take our chin in one hand and guide our line of vision. If we are totally exhausted by our foolish efforts, he has a chance of getting through to us. With his other hand he points a divine finger and says quietly, "There. Do you see it now?"

"Where? Is that it?" we ask, still desperately trying to remain in control.

But finally, finally, we see it and then all we can say is "Aha." There is not much more to say, because it rarely looks like we thought it would, and our understanding fills us less with pride than humility.

"Aha."

It is a rush of air out of our lungs that leaves us totally spent. And then, if we are wise enough, we say "Amen," for a sacred chapter has been closed.

God never says "Aha." He has no need of it in his vocabulary. He is never seeking understanding or being surprised by its arrival. He is always sitting in the first row of the balcony, watching intently as the players enter on cue, or late, knowing which understudy will gain the limelight and which star will blow a line. He watches it all, needing no playbill, knowing exactly which scene will turn a comedy into a tragedy. He watches and he waits, not for the climax or for the curtain call. He waits and waits through the intermissions, sitting patiently, perhaps with some anticipation, until finally, finally, one of the actors

189

breaks character, looks to the audience, and says, "Aha! Now I understand. This is not for us. This is for you." And then, I think, he claps.

We all realized at different points that Isabel was dying. For me it came the day she mentioned the possibility of a bone marrow transplant. Lively, vivacious Isabel, who had always painted life with great, bright brush strokes, described the procedure to me in uncharacteristic detail. It was as if she had centered in on a small portion of the canvas, and she was painting it carefully with a very fine brush. If she did this correctly, maybe she'd have more to paint in the future.

When the chemotherapy began to lose the race with the cancer that was devastating her body, Isabel began to talk about the bone marrow transplant.

"It's a radical procedure," she said. (The wife of a doctor, she always used proper terms, even when describing what they would do to her.) "They literally take you to the point of death before they can bring you back to life again," she said. We both thought about that for a moment, neither saying what we thought. Isabel was closer to death at that moment than either one of us knew. But the thought of entering this near-death state voluntarily made me shiver.

She never made it to the bone marrow transplant. She was gone two weeks after that conversation. I would be lying if I said that I had any understanding of why Isabel died. It is a raw and bleeding wound that rips open every time I see her young children.

But just as my own chapter of grief over Isabel opened, I felt the Lord's hands on my shoulder and the gentle turning. I thought of Isabel's careful description of the bone marrow transplant, and then I sighed. "Aha."

It had taken me years to see it, but now it was clear. God had taken me through the spiritual equivalent of a bone marrow transplant. He took me deep, deep into despair, almost to the point of death. He had to rip my self-righteousness away, purge my system of all my ideas of what was holy. Then, only then, could he infuse new life into my bones. Only then could he give me hope for a longer life to come. Only then could he show me what it was that he'd been hoping I'd see on my own. I heard his clapping, and I bowed my head.

"Amen," I said.

I would spend more days crying for Isabel, but I would never shed another tear for that woman I had left behind. It had been a painful procedure, but it was worth it. For me, it meant new life.

25

Growing Up

I HAD VIEWED THE SAME SCENE on television. But this time it was me in the hospital waiting room, watching the clock, looking up anxiously every time a doctor walked out of the corridor that lead to the operating room. On television the waiting was condensed to a few minutes. In reality it took hours.

"Is there any word on Mr. Hanson?" I finally asked the nurse.

"I'm sorry, but his operation has been delayed because of an emergency," the nurse said after checking her records. I sat back down with my mother and sister and waited for news about the man who had been the rock of each of our lives. It was still such a shock to think of my father, my healthy, jovial, father, suddenly ailing. He should be here to take charge of the situation. He should be reassuring us, telling us what to do. He was the one we had always leaned on. Now we were trying to hold ourselves together as we awaited word on him.

I did not know how to put a name to what I was feeling. I wanted desperately to do something, anything.

But all I could do was wait. I tried to pray, but all I could do was cry out to God, "Not Daddy. Please don't take Daddy." I still needed him so much, even as a grown woman. I wasn't ready for God to take him away from me. It was a totally selfish cry that reduced me to a child. What would I do if something happened to Daddy?

He had raised me to be an independent woman. He had encouraged me to achieve, to excel. He had helped me set goals and challenged me to exceed them. He had listened carefully to my ideas and teased me with questions that made me stretch my mind further. But mostly he had loved me, even when I fell short. He always found ways to let me know that he was there for me. Just a few months before, when I was staying at my parents home, he had stopped me on my way out the door and hugged me.

"You look beautiful," he said. His words filled me with confidence somewhere deep inside, where no one else could reach me. No matter what happened, I knew I could always go to my dad.

But now Daddy's life was hanging in the balance. The tumor the doctor had discovered in his brain was large. It was already pressing on important areas, making him lose his balance, causing terrible headaches. Daddy couldn't take care of anyone with this horrible thing growing in his head.

The doctor had tried to be encouraging. Perhaps it was benign, he offered. But I knew that he had little confidence in his own words. Only the biopsy would tell us the truth.

Hours passed. I began to think of all of the times that Daddy had been there for me. When I was a little girl and liked my shoelaces tied extra tight, only Daddy knew how to do them just right. I thought of his big hands fumbling with the laces on my little shoes. *Why did he respect my strange request every day?* I wondered. *Why did he put up with my odd quirks?*

I thought of the time I had begged him to let me go to the junior high school dance, even though our church frowned on dancing.

"I believe it's wrong," he had said. "But if you really want to go, I'll take you."

So Daddy and I had gone to the dance long enough for me to see the boy I had a crush on slow-dancing with another girl. He hugged me as I sobbed that night, without a hint of "I told you so."

I remembered the night I had called him from college. "I'm tired, Dad. I need to take some time off."

He had listened carefully to my plans to travel with a girlfriend instead of starting the next quarter of school. And then after a question or two, he had given me permission. "But be careful," he had said.

And then there was the night, less than a year ago, when he had driven me to the airport one evening to pick up my rental car. He had insisted on waiting for me at the curb and making sure I got into my car.

"I travel by myself all of the time," I had protested.

"I know you do," he had said. "But as long as I can do anything about it, I want to be sure you're all right. I'll never stop being your Dad, you know."

I didn't let him see the tear in my eye as I hugged him. He'd taught me to be independent, but we both knew better.

When my mother had called me to tell me that he had a brain tumor, I knew that Daddy would want me to be strong for Mom. I tried not to cry. I tried to be strong and organized. But as I sat in the hospital waiting room I knew that my charade couldn't last forever.

The door swung open and this time it was the surgeon we knew walking out. He came to where we sat and pulled a chair over.

"He's resting comfortably," he began.

I knew that bad news would follow.

"But I'm sorry to tell you that the tumor is malignant."

The word struck me with searing intensity.

"Can you remove it?" I asked hopefully.

The doctor looked grim as he explained the position of the tumor and the damage that would be caused by an operation.

"I'm sorry," he said with a finality that shook me. He stood up to walk away, and I stood too. I waited until we were out of my mother's hearing.

"How much time does he have?" I asked. "I have to know. I'll need to take care of things."

"A few months," he offered. "Maybe a year, although he wouldn't be in very good shape if he lived that long. I wouldn't count on more than a couple of months."

I thanked the doctor and leaned against the wall of the corridor. A few months to help Daddy take care of his business. A few months to say goodbye. A few months to grow up.

"I'm not ready, God," I said. "I will never be ready."

26

Taken By Surprise

I HAVE TO CONFESS THAT I'M NOT sure I ever really believed in miracles. At least not until now. Of course
I'd heard people say, "It's a miracle!" But usually I
took that to mean that the odds had been against
something, and it had happened anyway. The first
time a heart transplant worked it had been a miracle.
But now it is a routine procedure. What once was
miraculous becomes mundane.

Or I had watched faith healers report that diseases
were cured, or blind people saw after twenty years.
"Sure," the cynic in me would say. "It was probably
just a mistake in the first place."

It's not that I didn't believe in God. I knew he had
done a miracle in my own life. I had watched in awe
as he had taught me lessons, opening my heart and
mind to his presence.

I guess it's just that I hadn't seen God intervene
supernaturally in ways that defied the laws of nature. I
knew he could. I guess I didn't believe he did in my
world. Because if I believed he did intervene, then I'd

have to deal with the fact that at times he didn't. And that brought me back to questions like why God allows babies and mothers of small children to die. I had asked God for miracles and been disappointed. So I guess I had been afraid to ask anymore.

But now I have witnessed a miracle. A bona fide, outside-the-realm-of-understanding miracle. My father's brain tumor, once large and malignant and life-threatening, has simply disappeared. The doctors say it couldn't happen. But their own tests say otherwise. They are more than perplexed. They never say "cured." That's too much of an understatement for what has happened.

Over the months I had little by little given in to the idea that my father was dying. The doctors were pessimistic. The literature on the subject depressing. And I had begun to realize that bad things do happen to even the best people. Even men like my father who had spent a too-short lifetime looking out for others.

"He's such a good man," so many people observed. "Why has this happened to him?" With grace and calm, Daddy accepted the diagnosis, practically thinking of others as he got his affairs in order. When someone would call to tell him they were praying, he would get tears in his eyes.

"I can't believe so many people care," he would say, not realizing how his investment of years was coming back to him.

Then just as I braced myself for the blow I expected, a different blow came. Not the shock of tragedy, but the greater shock of a miracle. Not a defying-the-odds miracle. An it-can't-happen miracle. Daddy's life was spared by God's supernatural intervention.

When I tell people about this turn of events, some are immediately delighted. "Praise the Lord!" they exclaim. Others respond as I did when I first heard the news. "You're kidding," they say in disbelief. "Are you sure?"

I understand the second response better than the first. I awaken every morning grateful, but afraid. *What if it's a mistake?* And then I feel guilty. "Help thou my unbelief," I pray.

Miracles, I have found, are remarkably close to tragedies. They hit with the same numbing intensity. And they lead to the same inevitable questions: "Why my father and not hers? Was it because of our prayers or my father's belief? What about the others who prayed and believed, but are gone?"

I acknowledge to God that I believe he is sovereign, but then I seek to understand just some piece of this puzzle. I need to make sense of it, just as I want to believe that there was a reason that my friend died or that the thousands of innocents died as a result of droughts in Africa.

Why did it happen? And why can't I just be thankful? I struggle with this just as I struggle with tragedy. My faith, my beliefs are shaken by God being God. What does this say about my faith?

I have learned that I should "pray in faith, believing . . ." But mostly I realize that I pray in fear, hoping. Sometimes I pray in despair, doubting. Perhaps I have never really prayed in faith. Perhaps I have never truly believed.

I know these thoughts are human, but I struggle against my humanity. I wasn't ready for this gift, but God has given it to me anyway. He has rewarded my small mind and shallow faith with a miracle. He has shown me in his own magnificent way that I do not earn his love. He has reminded me that I am never ready for his surprises, even when I can almost hear him count, "1, 2, 3 . . ." I still jump when the surprise comes. I still despair in my limited ability to look directly at glory without turning away.

"God, help me to be more open," I pray. "I want you to be who you are, even if I don't understand it. Thank you for giving my father back to us. Now give me a faith big enough to rejoice in what I can't fathom."

Epilogue

Dear God,

I am a different person today than I was before I lost the baby. How strange it is that I look back at that loss and see it as a beginning. How odd that I still mourn my child but am not sorry for where that tragedy has brought me.

I do not like pain, but I no longer fear it. I do not enjoy the uncertainty of the future, but I move forward with a sense of calm. I am learning to step out into the future. I am learning to hold your hand.

In so many ways I feel like a child again. There's so much to learn, so many ways to want to grow. I need your guidance as I enter the next phase. Don't let me go backward. Help me grow into a woman of God. Help me be a daughter you can be proud of. Let people see the family resemblance between us.